100 GREATEST BASEBALL HEROES

BY MAC DAVIS

GROSSET & DUNLAP • PUBLISHERS • NEW YORK

About the Author

Mac Davis has been widely known as a sports storyteller. Readers of his many sports books number in the millions. But many more sport fans have heard his fascinating stories broadcast over hundreds of radio and television stations throughout the United States, Canada, and parts of Europe. Over the years, he has created and written many of the most popular sport shows ever presented on the air, hosted by some of the most famous sportscasters in America.

Other Sports Books by Mac Davis

100 GREATEST SPORTS HEROES

100 GREATEST SPORTS FEATS

THE GIANT BOOK OF SPORTS

TEEN-AGE BASEBALL LEGENDS

GREAT SPORTS HUMOR

THE GREATEST IN BASEBALL

BASEBALL'S UNFORGETTABLES

FOOTBALL'S UNFORGETTABLES

PACEMAKERS OF SPORTS

SPORTS SHORTS—AMAZING, STRANGE BUT TRUE

100 GREATEST FOOTBALL HEROES

LIBRARY OF CONGRESS CATALOG CARD NUMBER: 73-19192

ISBN: 0-448-11742-8 (TRADE EDITION)
ISBN: 0-448-13208-7 (LIBRARY EDITION)

Contents

The Wonderful World of Baseball

Ever since professional baseball began in America more than a century ago, countless boys and men have sought fame and fortune in big-league competition. Over the years, many achieved the glory of being idolized as heroes.

These pages tell the stories of the most magnificent heroes the game has ever known. Their incredible doings and amazing achievements encompass all the history, glories, legends and romance of America's national pastime. There never were greater baseball heroes than these.

Throughout this book, in brief but intimate biographies, the most fantastic ballplayers who ever made baseball history march in review. Also included are the game's outstanding pioneers, trailblazers, record makers, and monumental figures who shaped baseball into America's favorite sport.

This book will take fans of all ages on an exciting and fascinating journey through more than a hundred glorious baseball years, for a meeting with the most colorful, most fabulous, most remarkable baseball heroes who ever lived.

100 Greatest Baseball Heroes is an invitation to all baseball buffs for a most rewarding adventure in the wonderful world of baseball.

Mac Davis

FLY HAWKS IN THE OUTFIELD

BABE RUTH
The One and Only

No baseball hero ever did as much for America's national pastime as Babe Ruth. When the game was in its darkest hour, on the verge of ruin, he saved major-league baseball. No fictional story was ever more incredible than the true saga of baseball's most glamorous figure.

Born in Baltimore, Maryland, the son of a saloon keeper, George Herman Ruth began life in sordid poverty as an unwanted pushed-around nobody. When he was hardly eight years old, he was already a wild tough kid roaming the slum streets of Baltimore's waterfront, scratching for food, fighting and stealing. Tragedy came for him early in life. His mother suddenly died, and not long afterward, his father was murdered.

The neglected youngster was picked off the streets by police and sent to St. Mary's Industrial School, a charity refuge for homeless boys, orphans, and delinquents that was maintained by a religious order. There young Ruth was

taught right from wrong, the tailoring trade, and how to play baseball. He became so skilled a pitcher that a kindly brother from the school persuaded Jack Dunn, then the owner and manager of the minor-league Baltimore Orioles, to hire Ruth as a player for $600 a season. The owner had to adopt Ruth and become his legal guardian. His teammates called him Dunn's Babe, and "Babe" became Ruth's nickname for the rest of his life.

He was 19 years old when he crashed the big leagues as a pitcher for the Boston Red Sox. He was moon-faced, stood six-feet-two, packed 191 pounds on thin legs, and ran with funny little mincing steps. But he quickly became outstanding. In his first three full seasons, he won 64 games, and so superb and vital was his hurling for the Red Sox that in the six seasons he pitched for them they won their first three pennants. In World Series combat, pitcher Ruth distinguished himself as a winner and record-maker by hurling 29 consecutive scoreless innings. Curiously, while winning fame as a top pitcher of the majors, Babe Ruth became a home-run specialist as a pinch hitter. Eventually, his bat lost him his job on the mound, for he was persuaded to become an outfielder so that he would be in the daily lineup and play in every game. Babe Ruth became one of the game's greatest right fielders. He was a speedy, sure-handed fly hawk, never made a bad play, and was a crafty base runner.

In 1919, when he clouted 29 home runs—an unprecedented feat at that time—he became an idol for the whole baseball world. The following year, when Babe Ruth was 25, the Boston Red Sox ran into financial trouble, and

sold him to the New York Yankees for $125,000 in cash and a $350,000 loan.

In that year, big-league baseball was adversely affected by a scandal that almost destroyed the game. It was discovered that eight famous stars of the mighty pennant-winning Chicago White Sox team had conspired to "throw" the 1919 World Series, for a price, which they did. The scandal brought America's national pastime to an all-time low in public esteem. But colorful Babe Ruth, with his oversized bat, won fans back to the game. They flocked in droves to the ballparks to see "the Babe" hit his mighty home runs, and he never let them down.

In the 1920 season, he performed the unbelievable by belting 54 home runs. The following season he improved on the impossible feat by hitting 59 home runs. Only he ever hit 50 or more homers in a season—four times. Apprehensive pitchers walked him 2,056 times, for an all-time record.

He was the first player ever to hit 40 or more homers a season, eleven times. Thirteen times he was the home-run champion of the majors. Only he ever hit two home runs in a game 73 times! In 1927, when he collected 60 home runs in 154 major-league games, it was a feat for the ages. In his 22 seasons in the majors, the incredible Babe slugged 714 home runs, 15 in World Series play.

He did even more than that as baseball's most remarkable slugger. In 2,503 major-league games, and 8,399 times at bat, Babe Ruth made 2,873 hits, scored 2,174 runs, drove in 2,209 runs, and wound up with a lifetime batting average of .343—eighth highest in the record books. Moreover, in the 15 years he starred for the New York Yankees, he sparked them to seven pennants and six World Series championships.

He became the game's highest-salaried performer, drawing a higher annual salary than the President of the United States. His popularity throughout the nation and the world exceeded any other in the annals of the sport. At the height of his fame, the rollicking and carefree Babe received more than 20,000 fan letters a week from his worshipful admirers.

No other baseball hero ever had such a grip on the affection of youngsters as did lovable Babe Ruth. He was the most accessible and friendliest of them all, with a grin and a handshake for everybody.

In his glorious golden years he was never too busy to visit hospital wards to spread comfort and cheer. He had a genuine concern for youngsters. Once, before a World Series game, he visited a dying boy who begged him to hit a home run that afternoon especially for him. Ruth promised. And he did better than that to help that sick boy recover his health and live. He hit *three* home runs in that one World Series game, for an all-time record. No wonder Babe Ruth became a legend in his lifetime.

Babe Ruth was a weary 40 when he quit the majors as a player. He went out like a true champion. In his final game he belted three home runs as a farewell to glory. He left behind him an astonishing total of seventy-six baseball records, most of which are still unsurpassed.

He was the most famous, most colorful, most glamorous immortal ever to be enshrined in baseball's Hall of Fame. When he died on August 16, 1948, at the age of only 53, he was still the greatest hero in the baseball world. Millions of people from all walks of life mourned for him. He lay in state in the vast Yankee Stadium, known as "The House That Ruth Built," and more than 200,000 fans filed past his bier for a farewell glance at the superman whose thundering home runs saved big-league baseball from ruin, and altered the character and structure of America's national pastime.

More than any man, fabulous Babe Ruth made major-league baseball what it is today. He did the most for baseball.

TY COBB

The Georgia Peach

Ty Cobb was the strangest baseball hero in history. Though he stands alone in his glory as a fiery genius and the greatest major-league player who ever lived, he was the most hated player who ever made imperishable baseball history.

During his turbulent 24 seasons in the majors, he performed incredible feats beyond the reach of the game's

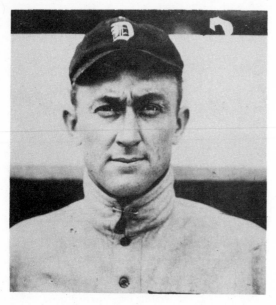

the Detroit Tigers of the American League. He was a brazen, arrogant and conceited rookie, driven by a wild fury to become the greatest ballplayer ever. He came late in the 1905 season, played in 41 games, and was something of a bust as a rookie. He batted a mere .240 for his debut.

But then the "Georgia Peach," as he came to be known, suddenly ripened, and Ty Cobb never hit less than .320 during the next 21 years of play for the Detroit Tigers, and in his final two years playing for the Philadelphia Athletics. During those last two seasons, though he was past 40, he batted a mere .357 and .323 for his fame.

When Ty Cobb was racing to baseball immortality, he was such a mean and bad loser that he became the game's most awesome winner. He dominated a game from the first to the last inning. Always, he had the opposition nonplussed, because they were at a loss as to how to play him. He did everything different—at bat, on the field, and on the base paths.

With his daring, insight, and trickiness, the "Georgia Peach" bewildered batteries and upset infields. He could score from first on a single, go from first to third on a sacrifice bunt, or score from second on infield outs or short sacrifice flies to the outfield. Sometimes, he stole all three bases in an inning. One season, fleet-footed Ty stole 96 bases, and only he ever stole a lifetime total of 892 bases—an all-time record that may never be equaled.

He never gave an infielder or catcher more than the tip of his toe to tag. He developed the fadeaway, fallaway, and hook slides for subsequent base-stealers to use for their larceny fame. The six-

best, but he never had a friend to call his own. Most of his teammates and all rival players feared and hated him for his burning desire to excel in everything. He had a legion of enemies always plotting his downfall. Among the game's fans he aroused such violent antagonism that he often required police protection. A would-be assassin once attacked him with a knife and almost killed him. Another time, a mob tried to kidnap him—to lynch him. Ty Cobb nonetheless remained the fieriest and angriest competitor, playing in each of his 3,033 major-league games as if it was a matter of life or death.

Born in Narrows, Georgia, Tyrus Raymond Cobb came, surprisingly, from a gentle and cultured Southern family. His father was a mayor, a state senator, and a scholarly educator. Young Cobb was expected to enter West Point. But, much to his father's dismay and disapproval, Ty embraced a professional baseball career at the age of seventeen.

At 18, he came to the big leagues as a $700 purchase to play center field for foot, 175-pound "Georgia Peach" slashed more infielders with his flashing spikes in quest of base-stealing glory than any other player—but he could take it, as well as dish it out, in the violence of diamond warfare.

As a spectacular center fielder, he had few peers. He was a magnificent fly hawk with a powerful throwing arm to nip runners. But when it came to the art of hitting, he had no equal, and never will. He was the absolute limit as a batsman genius.

In 11,429 times at bat in major-league games, the incredible Ty Cobb produced 724 doubles, 297 triples, 118 homers, and 3,052 singles, to amass an unbelievable lifetime total of 4,191 safe hits. No other player ever came close to 4,000 hits.

Only the fantastic "Georgia Peach" ever won a major-league batting championship 12 times—nine times in a row. Among his other feats for glory: he scored 2,244 runs, batted in 1,954, and collected 6,394 putouts. He wound up with a lifetime batting average of .367

—the highest ever achieved. It's a major-league record that will stand unmatched forever. When Ty Cobb left the big leagues as a player, at the age of 43, he had established more baseball records than any other: one hundred!

No wonder, then, that when baseball's Hall of Fame was built at Cooperstown as an eternal pantheon for the gods of the game, Ty Cobb was the very first one chosen to enter. For, as usual, he had to be first in everything.

Curiously, as baseball's greatest player grew old, he mellowed and tried to recast his one-time poor public image by using his wealth for good deeds. He set up an educational foundation to provide college scholarships and financial aid for needy and worthy young students. Also, he built a hospital for his home town.

Even when he departed from this world in 1961, at the age of 75, Ty Cobb was still unique. He died as the wealthiest former baseball player of all time, leaving an estate of fourteen million dollars.

WILLIE MAYS

The "Say Hey" Kid

William Howard Mays was born to play baseball. From the moment of his birth on May 6, 1931, in Westfield, Alabama, his destiny was set. When he was still in his cradle, his first

toy was a baseball. At the age of three, he was given his first baseball glove. His father, grandfather, and uncle, who had been one-time pro baseball players, could hardly wait for Willie to grow

up so that they could start teaching and coaching him how to catch, field and hit. He was only six when his lessons began. Before he was fourteen, Willie was already playing semi-pro ball with a baseball team of grown men.

In 1951, on his twentieth birthday, Willie Mays suddenly found himself in the big leagues as the centerfielder for the New York Giants of the National League. With only 116 minor-league games behind him, Willie was a frightened and bewildered rookie. When he made only one safe hit in his first twenty-six times at bat, he became so discouraged that he pleaded tearfully with his manager to send him back to the minor leagues where he had been a sensation. But the tough, hard-boiled Giants' pilot, Leo ("Lippy") Durocher, merely laughed and told the unhappy black youngster:

"You let me do the worrying, Willie. You belong in the majors and that's where you'll stay for a long time. You're my centerfielder, and I need you to win a pennant."

So, rookie Willie Mays remained, and in his first season he blossomed into such a magnificent all-around player that he inspired, sparked and paced the Giants to their most miraculous pennant triumph. He emerged from that memorable season as a runaway winner of the coveted Rookie of the Year Award. Such was the beginning of the Willie Mays legend.

There were no pennants for the New York Giants the following two seasons, because Willie was no longer playing center field for them. He was away in the United States Army. But no sooner had he returned, in 1954, than once again his brilliant playing inspired, sparked and paced the Giants to a pennant, and even more—to a four-game sweep of the World Series championship. In that post-season classic, Willie made some of the most unbelievable outfield catches ever seen.

As the years passed, the ever-laughing, bubbling, happy "Say Hey" Kid, as he came to be nicknamed (because he never remembered names, and always hailed everyone that way), grew to awesome status. He became the most colorful, most exciting, and most spectacular major-league player of his time. His feats on the diamond were simply incredible.

He became the first player in history to hit more than 300 home runs and steal more than 300 bases. Six times he hit more than 40 home runs in a season, and twice he hit more than 50. He became the ninth player in history to hit four home runs in a nine-inning game, and the ninth player in history to collect more than 3,000 safe hits. He also became the second player in history to hit more than 600 home runs. Often his impossible catches in the outfield defied belief. Also, he became the only player in history to win the Most Valuable Player Award, eleven years apart. Eighteen times he was chosen to play in the annual All-Star Game between the greatest players in the two major leagues, and often he was its outstanding star. Three times he sparked the Giants to pennants.

Willie Mays became the most loved and admired baseball hero of his time, the idol of countless millions of people, young and old.

The legend of the fabulous "Say Hey" Kid finally came to an end at the close of the 1973 season, when Willie Mays retired as a player at the age of 42. By then, he had earned about $2,000,000 from baseball.

He left behind an awesome record for his baseball immortality. He had played in 2,992 major-league games, gone to bat 10,881 times, made 3,283 hits, belted 140 triples, 523 doubles, and 660 home runs—to bat in 1,963 runs, and score 2,062 runs himself. He also made 7,740 putouts, stole almost 400 bases, and wound up with a .302 lifetime batting average.

Willie Mays left behind him the legend of a superstar baseball hero that will stand out like a beacon for all to see and marvel at through the ages.

STAN MUSIAL

Stan the Man

At 17, he became a professional baseball player. At 19, he was a dead-armed washed-up pitcher in the minor leagues. At 21, he became an outfielder in the big leagues where he was to remain for twenty-two glorious years. At 43, he left the major leagues idolized as an immortal folk hero of the baseball world. For Stan Musial it all began on a river of tears.

Born in the drab steel-mill town of Donora, Pennsylvania, the son of a poor Polish immigrant laborer, Stanley Frank Musial yearned from early boyhood to become a famous baseball player. When only 17, he had to make an important decision for his future. As a high school graduate, he had been

offered a college scholarship for his outstanding athletic skills. His father insisted that he go to college for an education. But young Stan wanted to become a professional baseball player, instead. He had received an offer from a minor-league club to pitch for sixty-five dollars a month.

Father and son argued for a long time. When Stanley's oratory failed to convince his adamant father, he began to cry. He cried so hard that it reduced both his father and mother to tears. The three cried up a river of tears.

Finally, Papa Musial relented and said: "For my son I wanted a better and easier life than I have had. But if baseball playing means so much to you, I won't stand in your way."

At 17, Stan Musial became a professional pitcher, but he was less than dazzling as a minor-league hurler. One day, he fell and badly injured his left shoulder and pitching arm. At only 19, he became an unwanted pitcher with no baseball future.

A kindly and wise minor-league manager came to his rescue from oblivion. He advised 20-year-old Musial to become an outfielder. A year later, Stan was in the big leagues as a rookie for the St. Louis Cardinals. From the start he performed as if he were destined for greatness. He fielded spectacularly in left field, and he batted .315. It was the beginning of a glorious record-breaking 22-year stay with the St. Louis Cardinals, during which time he established himself as one of the game's foremost candidates for Hall of Fame immortality.

In his sophomore year in the majors, Musial, already dubbed "Stan the Man," really began to blaze as an in-comparable performer. He ran away with the National League batting championship, and from then on he would hit better than .300-plus for sixteen consecutive years. So devastating was he at bat, with his curious corkscrew stance, that eighteen times he topped the .300-plus mark, and seven times he won the National League batting championship.

With the passing seasons, "Stan the Man" performed incredible feats beyond the reach of all other baseball greats. Only he ever hit five home runs in a single day of major-league play. He achieved that feat during a double-header in the 1954 season, hitting three home runs in the first game and two homers in the second.

Astonishing and matchless was his durability. Only he ever played 100 or more games a season, twenty-one times. He was the only major-league player to log more than a thousand games at each of two positions—the outfield and first base. He made more long hits than any other player—1,377—and 475 of them were home runs.

Incredible Stan Musial played in more major-league games than anyone else in baseball history—3,026. He came to bat more times than anyone else—10,972. He collected for his fame 3,630 safe hits, scored more runs (1,949), and drove in more runs (1,951) than any other batter. He finished with a lifetime batting average of .331. His magnificent playing rewarded him with the coveted Most Valuable Player Award three times. And four times it sparked the St. Louis Cardinals to pennants.

But "Stan the Man" was more than a superlative player who created sixty different and separate all-time records in testimony of his greatness. Off the field, he was equally known for his modesty, sportsmanship, and gentlemanly conduct. He was idolized by millions of baseball fans, and admired by the nation's high and mighty. Four different United States Presidents welcomed him to the White House to bestow praise upon him.

He stimulated such affection from his legion of admirers that more than $50,000 was raised by public subscription to build a magnificent ten-foot bronze statue of "Stan the Man" in his famed batting crouch to stand at the entrance to the St. Louis Cardinals' ballpark. It was a unique honor.

No greater star now shines at baseball's Hall of Fame in Cooperstown than Stanley Frank Musial.

TED WILLIAMS

The Splendid Splinter

Ted Williams, the Boston Red Sox superslugger, was the greatest batsman the game saw in a generation.

He was something to see: Smoothly swinging his big bat, eying the pitcher with scorn, flawlessly meeting the ball with his superb wrist snap, following through with beautiful coordination of arms and body, he was indeed the picture hitter, with the additional attribute of having a camera eye. His list of hitting accomplishments was unmatched by anybody of his time.

He was the only .400 hitter in more than 40 years of big-league play. His lifetime batting average was the highest in a generation. His 521 home runs place him in the top eight on the all-time list. He won the batting championship six times, and was walked more often than any other player, with the exception of Babe Ruth, in the history of the game.

Ted accomplished all this despite injuries and despite Marine military serv-

ice which cost him the equivalent of six full seasons. There is no telling what kinds of fantastic marks he might have achieved if he could have played those extra seasons.

Yet, throughout his glorious career,

Williams was the most controversial player in the majors. He was temperamental, outspoken, highly sensitive, and often surly. He irked club owners, managers, fans and sportswriters. Many times he was fined for his petulant behavior and angry public outbursts. Once he was hit with a $5,000 fine for a rude display—the highest fine of its kind in baseball history.

There are those who believe that this arrogance could be traced to his unhappy childhood. Born in San Diego, California, Theodore Samuel Williams was a product of a broken home, and nothing came easy. His mother, a bonneted Salvation Army worker who was known locally as "Salvation May," had dedicated him to the Salvation Army when he was still a baby. But Ted's boyhood dream was of becoming a famous big-league hitter and outfielder. Or pitcher.

As a gangling 17-year-old—6-foot-4 and only 146 pounds—he signed with the San Diego Padres of the Pacific Coast League. He was a pitcher then, but when his first manager saw him in the batter's box, that was changed immediately. He became an outfielder. Ted was so thin that one baseball scout, well-meaning, told his mother: "Mrs. Williams, if you let that boy of yours play pro ball, it will kill him!"

Three years later, after some minor-league polishing which Williams didn't think he needed, he broke into the majors as a left fielder for the Boston Red Sox. He wasted no time in becoming an outstanding performer. At the end of his first season in the big leagues, the 20-year-old kid had posted a .327 batting average, had hit 31 home runs,

had led the American League in runs batted-in, and had been acclaimed Rookie of the Year.

Now nicknamed "The Splendid Splinter," Williams became the toast of the baseball world. As a major-league sophomore, he hit .344, and then in 1941 he reached his peak as the greatest batter of his time. Cocky 23-year-old Ted Williams came down to the last day of that season with a magnificent batting average of exactly .400. On that final day, the Red Sox were to play a double-header. Old hands on that team advised young Ted to sit out the final two games to protect his phenomenal .400 batting mark. But Williams insisted on playing.

"I don't want anyone ever saying that I made my .400 batting average by hiding in the dugout. I don't want to win any batting championship while sitting on the bench. If I can't keep hitting, then I don't deserve the .400 mark."

Play he did, and on that memorable day he went to bat eight times, lashing out six hits, to close that season with a .406 batting average and win his first major-league batting title. He was the last player in American League history to bat .400.

The pell-mell rush of the "Splendid Splinter" to fame continued unabated. The following season, he not only won his second major-league batting championship, but he also won the "Triple Crown" of the majors—tops in batting, first in home runs hit, and tops in runs-batted-in.

After four of the most glorious seasons a big-league baseball hero ever had, Fate intervened and robbed left-fielder Ted Williams of three playing years in the majors. He joined the United States Marines as a fighter pilot in World War II.

When he finally returned to major-league baseball, he quickly reclaimed his fame as the greatest hitter in the game. Again he captured the coveted "Triple Crown," won two more league batting championships, twice won the Most Valuable Player Award, and set a slew of records before Fate intervened once more to halt his march on the glory road to baseball immortality. Ted Williams was recalled to military service, at 34, to fly a fighter plane in the Korean War.

Miraculously, the "Splendid Splinter" escaped death a few times, and after losing almost three more playing seasons, he returned to the majors.

At 39, he astonished the baseball world by winning another batting championship, to become the oldest player in big-league history for such a feat. So, the following year, at 40, Ted Williams again amazed the baseball world by winning his sixth major-league batting championship.

In 1960, at age 42, Ted Williams finally quit as a major-league player, and he went out in a blaze of glory, befitting the glamorous baseball hero he was. In his final game and final time at bat, he clouted the longest home run he had ever hit in his lifetime total of 521. He had played in 2,292 major-league games, had made 2,654 hits, 1,798 runs, driven in 1,839, and wound up with a lofty lifetime batting average of .341.

"All I want out of life," said Ted Williams when he first reached the big leagues, "is that when I walk down the street, folks will say 'There goes the greatest hitter who ever lived!'" He came mighty close to that goal. For no star now in baseball's Hall of Fame outshines immortal Ted Williams.

WILLIE KEELER

"Hit 'Em Where They Ain't"

No little man ever accomplished as much in baseball and went as far on the road to fame as William ("Wee Willie") Keeler. In big-league livery he stood only sixty-four inches tall and tipped barely 135 pounds with bat in hand.

Born in Brooklyn, the son of a horse-car driver, Willie was twenty when he made his first appearance in a big-league game in 1892. The New York club of the National League had paid $800 for his bush-league contract. When the umpire spied tiny Willie com-

ing to home plate for his first lick as a batter, he thought a joke was being played on him.

"Get that bat boy off the field!" ordered the ump.

"That's not our bat boy," snapped the Giants' pilot. "He's our new shortstop."

In his first two seasons in the majors, Wee Willie played with no success, and he was used sparingly as an infielder. But in 1894, when he was shipped off to the Baltimore Orioles and they turned him into their right fielder, the smallest player in the big leagues was off and flying.

Wee Willie made 200 or more hits in each of eight consecutive seasons, and for thirteen full seasons he never hit below .300. A left-handed swinger, he compiled batting averages almost beyond belief: .367, .376, .379, .392, and

.394; his highest batting mark for a season was .432!

It took outstanding baseball greats to match or break Keeler's records. One season he made 243 hits, and for more than a decade it remained an all-time mark. Once he set the pace for consistent batting by hitting safely in forty-four consecutive major-league games, a record that stood unbroken for forty-four years. His record of hitting 202 singles in the 1898 season still stands.

That diminutive Irishman became famous and feared as the player who "hit 'em where they ain't." He could bunt any time he chose. Once, he went through an entire season without striking out. As an outfielder, he was a speedy, sure-handed fly hawk, and on the base paths he was a tricky and clever burglar. One season he swiped seventy-three bases.

Wherever he played, pennants followed. He was on five championship teams. Although he was extremely shy and modest, he nevertheless became so famous in that tough swashbuckling baseball era that he was one of the first to command a five-figure salary for a season.

In his nineteen years in the majors, pint-sized Willie played in 2,124 games, was at bat 8,564 times, made 2,955 hits, scored 1,720 runs, and wound up with a lifetime batting average of .345 —the fifth highest in baseball history.

Wee Willie was almost forty when he played his final major-league game. The tiniest player in big-league history wound up a diamond giant—an immortal of the game. He is the smallest member in baseball's Hall of Fame.

MEL OTT

The Boy Who Grew Up in the Big Leagues

Though he stood only sixty-nine inches tall, Mel Ott, in his twenty-two spectacular years as a major-league outfielder, was one of the most awesome sluggers in the history of the game. In all, he clouted 511 career home runs. He also played right field with such finesse that everywhere he was known as "Mr. Right Field."

Melvin Thomas Ott was only a 16-year-old baby-faced country boy from Gretna, Louisiana, when he first came to the big leagues to play for the New York Giants. He fancied himself a catcher. But their fabled manager, John McGraw, thought that Ott was too small to make it as a backstop in the big time, even though he was a natural hitter destined for greatness. So, one day, McGraw said:

"Hey, Ott, you ever play the outfield?"

"Only when I was a kid," answered the 16-year-old youngster. Manager McGraw had to restrain himself from laughing.

Nevertheless, Ott was turned into an outfielder. But McGraw thought his new boy-player was too valuable to be entrusted to a minor-league team for seasoning, so from the first day on that Ott came to the Giants, he was and remained for twenty-two years a major-leaguer. Manager McGraw brought him along slowly, always having the youngster sit next to him in the dugout to absorb some of his baseball wisdom, and at times sending him into a game in the late innings to play right field. He watched over him, protected and guided him, as if he were his son. Within two seasons, Ott became the Giants' regular right fielder, hitting 18 homers and batting .322, while fielding his out-field position faultlessly. In his fourth season in the majors, 20-year-old Ott really burst out as a superstar. He hit a gaudy total of 42 homers, drove in 151 runs, and batted .328.

From then on, "Ottie," as a legion of admiring fans affectionately called him, was one of the most feared sluggers in the game's history, leading his league in homers six times. The chunky 170-pound right fielder performed heroics so often with timely game-winning home runs that prudent pitchers, wary of letting him have a crack at the ball, walked him whenever they could. He became so feared a slugger that ten times he collected more than a hundred bases-on-balls a season. Six times he was the league's most walked batter. Only he, in major-league history, was walked five times in five times at bat, in each of four games. He was walked more times than any other player in National League history—1,700 times.

Ott collected a bushel of records for his fame as an unforgettable baseball hero. He was the first modern major-league player to score six runs in a nine-inning game, and achieved that astonishing feat twice. Only he, in National League history, hit two home runs in one game—49 times. He set league records for runs scored, runs-batted-in, and extra-base hits. In all, he played in 2,730 major-league games, made 2,876 safe hits, and wound up with a batting average of .300-plus.

The fabulous "Mr. Right Field" didn't get into a World Series until his eighth season in the majors, 1933. He celebrated that happy occasion by starting with a home run the first time he came to bat, and dramatically end-ing that World Series classic with a winning home run in the final inning of the last game, to make the New York Giants baseball champions of the world. He subsequently sparked the Giants to two more consecutive pen-nants.

When Ott had aged to 33, he became the playing-manager of the New York Giants, and remained their pilot for seven years.

Such was the glorious saga of the boy who actually grew up in the big leagues for his imperishable fame as a baseball hero. Shortly after Mel Ott had completed his 22-year career in the majors, he was given the ultimate testi-monial of his true greatness as a major-league super ballplayer. He was en-shrined in the Hall of Fame, ever to be honored as an immortal of the game.

But the amazing Mel Ott, destined to baseball greatness from boyhood, was also destined to tragedy. At 49, he was killed in a terrible automobile collision on a foggy road in Mississippi. The en-tire baseball world mourned him.

In Ott's home town of Gretna, Lou-isiana, the green grass of the Mel Ott Park, a beautiful park dedicated in his honor, now keeps alive the memory of one of baseball's finest heroes.

JOE DiMAGGIO

The Yankee Clipper

Joseph Paul DiMaggio actually became a baseball player and went on to big-league immortality because he didn't like fishing.

Born in Martinez, California, the son of an Italian immigrant fisherman who wanted all of his sons to follow in his footsteps, young Joe rebelled against his father's expectations. He hated fishing, and the roll of a boat and the smell of dead fish made him ill. To escape it, he began playing baseball on the sandlots of North Beach in San Francisco, sold newspapers, and, as a teenager, signed to play with an industrial baseball team.

He was 18 when his mother helped him realize part of his baseball dreams. She persuaded stern Papa DiMaggio to permit Joe to accept an offer to play professional baseball for the San Francisco Seals of the Pacific Coast League.

In his first season of minor-league baseball, Joe was a sensation. He not only hit .340 as a spectacular center fielder, and drove in an unbelievable 169 runs, but he also made minor-league history by hitting safely in 61 consecutive games. Big-league baseball scouts eyed him hungrily.

Before he could get to the big

leagues, however, DiMaggio suffered the first of many injuries which were to plague his career—but never dim it. He cracked a knee in a freak accident, and all of the major-league scouts who had been following him shied away. Except the Yankees' scout. The New York club took a chance on him for a purchase price of $25,000, probably the biggest bargain in baseball history.

He arrived in New York in 1936, age 21, and in his rookie year slashed out

206 hits, worth a .323 batting average. He drove in 125 runs. His graceful, effortless fielding and base running were superb. The shy youngster became not only the idol of boys and grown men throughout the country, but an inspiration to his teammates. In his 13 years with the New York Yankees, they won ten pennants and nine World Series championships.

His feats are legion. Three times he was chosen Most Valuable Player. He was annually picked for the American League All-Star game. In 1937 he smacked 46 home runs, his career high, and that same year he drove in 167 runs. But his greatest conquest was still to come.

That was in 1941. That season, magnificent center fielder Joe DiMaggio glowed as a glamorous baseball hero beyond compare. In a game on May 15th, the famed "Yankee Clipper" (as he had become known) went to bat and belted out a safe hit. It was not unusual for him to hit safely, for already he had won a couple of batting championships with such averages as .352 and .381. However, as he continued to hit safely thereafter, in game after game, the baseball world began to watch his hitting streak with feverish excitement. "Jolting Joe," as he was also nicknamed, continued to hit safely until he had carried his hitting streak past all the flagpoles erected by baseball's greatest hitters. Finally, when he was stopped in a game on July 17th of that season, the incredible DiMaggio had completed the longest and most unbelievable hitting streak ever achieved by a major-league player. He had hit safely in 56 consecutive games!

During his fantastic hitting streak, he had gone to bat 223 times, had belted 15 homers, four three-baggers, 16 doubles, and 56 singles, for a total of 91 hits. Also, he had batted in 55 runs, and personally scored 56 times. It was the most amazing batting accomplishment of all time, and the one baseball feat least likely ever to be equaled.

As if that wasn't enough hitting glory for the "Yankee Clipper," the very next day after his unbelievable long hitting streak had been stopped, he began a new hitting streak that stretched to 16 games in a row. The fabulous Joe DiMaggio thus became the only major-league player in history ever to hit safely in 72 out of 73 consecutive games played in one season. The awesome feat helped the New York Yankees win the American League pennant by a margin of 17 games.

After the following season, wondrous Joe ·DiMaggio bid good-bye to his legion of admirers and went off to military service in World War II for three years.

When he returned to the major leagues in 1946, he was still a remarkably graceful and effortless performer at bat and the outfield, even though hobbled by a bone spur in his right heel. In his last five seasons in the majors, he sparked the Yankees to four pennants and four World Series championships.

By 1949, his bone spur was so painful that an operation was performed to alleviate the torture. Joe missed spring training and half of that season. But when he returned to the Yankee lineup, even though he hadn't seen a baseball thrown in major-league competition for eight months, he rose to the occasion, when needed, with such brilliance that baseball fans couldn't believe their eyes.

He batted .346, and his elegant fielding helped the Yankees win another pennant, then two more flags the following two seasons.

After the 1951 season, though Joe DiMaggio had been earning $100,000 a season (the first player to draw such an annual salary), the 37-year-old "Yankee Clipper" decided to retire as a major-league player, even though the New York club urged him to stay on. But the proud Joe DiMaggio felt that he could no longer give the baseball fans his magnificent best, and he left the game.

He left behind him an impressive record as a baseball hero.

In the 1,736 major-league games he had played, he had made 2,214 hits, hit 361 homers, scored 1,390 runs, batted in 1,537 runs, and wound up with a lifetime batting average of .325.

The gates of the Baseball Hall of Fame swung smoothly open for him—as smoothly, say, as he was remembered going back for a long fly to center field.

BILL HOY
The Amazing Dummy

The first physically handicapped player to achieve outstanding fame as a baseball hero was William Ellsworth Hoy from Houcktown, Ohio.

He popped up in 1888, when he was 24 years old, and remained an outfielder for fourteen exciting years, starring for five major-league clubs—Washington, Cincinnati, Louisville, St. Louis, and Chicago (1888-1902).

At the beginning of his career, the 65-inch, 150-pound Bill Hoy was unfairly regarded as some kind of freak. In childhood he had lost his hearing and speaking abilities because of a "brain fever" illness. But Bill Hoy wasted no time in showing the baseball world that he not only belonged in the big time, but that he was one of the brainiest outfielders ever seen in action. Few outfielders ever threw faster to bases to nip runners trying to stretch hits to the outfield than little Bill Hoy. He was a speedy sure-handed fly hawk in the field, and at bat a consistent and dangerous hitter. On the base paths he was an elusive thief, and came to be known as the "Amazing Dummy."

During his years in the big leagues, deaf-mute Hoy devised a system of signals to communicate with his teammates. He is also credited with working out the arm signals of umpires. Since he couldn't hear the calls of balls and strikes when he was at bat, he asked the plate umpire to raise his right arm to signify a strike. The signal became standard procedure with all big-league umpires, and remains to this day.

Baseball fans of that time also developed an interesting method of communicating their admiration of Hoy's prowess. Whenever he performed an important and outstanding play, the crowd in the stands would arise en masse and wildly wave arms and hats. Needless to say, Hoy merited many standing ovations.

In his brilliant 14-year big-league career, the "Amazing Dummy" played in 1,784 games, hit 236 doubles, 118 triples, and 41 homers, to finish with a lifetime total of 2,057 safe hits. He also scored 1,419 runs, and stole 605 bases.

Even when he departed from this world in 1961, he rated another unique distinction. He had been the oldest living ex-player in major-league baseball. When he died, Bill Hoy was one hundred years old.

TRIS SPEAKER
The Gray Eagle

Tristram E. Speaker was the most incredible, most spectacular, and greatest defensive center fielder in big-league history. His like will never be seen again.

In the era of the dead ball, he was able to play his center field position just beyond the infield. Time and again, he robbed batters of sure hits by spearing line drives that would have gone for singles. He nabbed sure-hit Texas League pop flies and caught runners off base for amazing double plays. If a batter took hold of a pitch and slammed a surprising long fly to the outfield over his head, he was equally amazing. He would race swiftly in pursuit of the ball, turn just at the right moment, and pull down the drive.

As evidence of Speaker's unique and

immortal in history (793), and as an added fillip to his greatness, he also stole 433 bases.

Tris Speaker was born in Hubbard City, Texas, and he was as much at home in the saddle on a bucking bronco as he was on a baseball field. He was a rodeo performer before he became a big-league player.

He was only 19 when he came to the major leagues, in 1907, to play for the Boston Red Sox. He had been bought for only $500. Within a year, he became the regular Red Sox center fielder, and for 19 consecutive years he played and starred in one hundred or more games a season. Seventeen times he hit better than .300. He sparked the Red Sox to two pennants and two World Series championships before they traded him to the Cleveland Indians for a large sum of money and several players. That was in 1916.

In Cleveland, where he starred brilliantly for the next eleven years, the "Gray Eagle" became an even more popular and greater baseball idol than ever before. He also became the Indians' playing manager. But he never grew stuffy nor too serious as a big-league pilot. He once spiced the opening day of a new baseball season with an unprecedented caper to show off his expert horsemanship. Before the start of that inaugural game, player-manager Speaker pulled on a pair of boots, hitched on fancy chaps, and strapped on spurs. As more than 40,000 fans gasped in astonishment, he then mounted a spirited horse which had been led into the ballpark by a cowboy, and raced it at full speed around the rim of the playing field. After his wild gallop, he dismounted and resumed his

remarkable ability in the outfield, he made more assists than any center fielder in history, 449—an all-time record that never has been even vaguely approached. He also set an all-time record of 35 assists in two separate seasons, a mark that still stands. And he set all-time records for most putouts, lifetime (6,706), and most chances accepted (7,195). He was the only center fielder in history who made two unassisted double plays in a season.

But it wasn't only incredible fielding that earned the "Gray Eagle" (he had both gray hair and speed) his honored place in baseball's Hall of Fame. In his twenty-two years in the major leagues he played in 2,789 games, was at bat 10,208 times, scored 1,881 runs, batted in 1,559 runs, and collected an astounding total of 3,515 safe hits, for a lifetime batting average of .344. He hit more doubles than any other baseball chores of playing and managing for the Indians.

Ironically, the greatest defensive center fielder in big-league history was indirectly responsible for causing the violent death of a teammate. At the end of the 1919 season, the Indians' brilliant shortstop, Ray Chapman, married a society girl and announced his retirement from baseball. Tris Speaker, however, persuaded the ten-year major-league veteran to change his decision and return to play just one more season. He needed Ray Chapman's fielding and hitting, for Speaker wanted to pilot the Indians to their first modern major-league pennant and World Series championship. As a special favor to his good friend, Ray Chapman consented.

By a cruel and tragic quirk of fate, Ray Chapman was fatally "beaned" by a fireball pitch late in that 1920 season, and became the first and only player to be killed in a major-league game.

It was a grief-stricken Tris Speaker who led the Cleveland Indians to the coveted World Series championship, to honor the memory of his lost friend. That season, player-manager Speaker hit .388 for his fame. But the season of his greatest glory was also the saddest triumph of his fabulous career.

MICKEY MANTLE

A Boy With a Mission

No sooner was Mickey Charles Mantle born in Spavinaw, Oklahoma, than he became a boy with a mission. His father, a humble zinc and lead miner who once had been an obscure semipro baseball pitcher, began to live with a dream. In his fantasy, Mutt Mantle saw his son as a famous big-league baseball player. (He had even named him in honor of his baseball idol, Hall-of-Fame catcher Mickey Cochrane.)

Mickey was only five years old when lessons in the art of baseball began. He began to learn how to catch and throw a baseball, and how to hit it with a bat.

No boy ever tried harder to please his father. The fear of failing in his father's eyes plagued Mickey throughout his boyhood.

As he grew older, Mickey became strong and muscular, and because he lived in football country, he mixed baseball playing with football. He became the star halfback for his high school football team. But his father never permitted him to forget that his mission was to make a father's dream of glory come true.

"You're not going to grub for a living in the mines, like me," his father often told him. "You're going to be-

come a famous big-league ballplayer."

So, Mickey drove himself fiercely to attain baseball perfection. He was still in high school when his ambitious father convinced a baseball scout for the then-famed New York Yankees to sign him up for a two-thousand dollar bonus.

But, one day, Mickey almost destroyed his father's dream forever. He was injured playing in a football game. To the young man's mental anguish and horror, doctors informed him that he was a victim of osteomyelitis, a bone disease afflicting his leg.

Nevertheless, at the age of 19, Mickey came to the major leagues to play center field for the New York Yankees. He was a powerful fleet-footed, and sure-handed rookie. But because of his leg affliction, he played with the constant fear that any baseball game might be his last. Whenever he played, his leg was heavily bandaged.

To add to his mental anguish, rookie Mantle learned that his father had become a victim of the dreaded Hodgkins disease that was eating away his life. Mutt Mantle lived long enough to see Mickey have a spectacular first season in the big leagues, hitting .311, belting 23 home runs, and helping the Yankees win a pennant. In his first World Series, Mickey delivered ten hits, including two homers.

Though he lost his father soon after, Mickey remained a baseball hero with a mission—to reach the diamond greatness his father had dreamed for him.

As the seasons passed, though his glory road was paved with pain, struggle and frustration, he gamely carried on for his mission. He suffered many injuries, and six times he had to undergo surgery on both legs so that he could continue to play. Courageously, he defied all his handicaps to perform astonishing feats as one of the best center fielders in baseball.

In 1956, he became the ninth player in history to win the coveted "Triple Crown" of the majors. He had a top batting average of .353, plus 130 runs-batted-in, and the most home runs for that season, 52.

Again and again, he led his league in fielding averages, slugging, and bases on balls. He became the most feared and greatest switch-hitter of home runs of all time, belting homers from both sides of home plate for such incredible distances that they had to be seen to be believed. In all, he hit 536 home runs for his major-league fame.

He became so versatile a center fielder that three times he was honored with the "Most Valuable Player" award. Also, he became so fabulous a star that he was the first player to be paid a season's salary of $100,000 for six successive years. Moreover, Mickey Mantle became a national baseball idol to millions of boys and grownups alike.

At the end of the 1968 season, when he was 38 years old, injury-scarred and pain-weary Mickey finally retired as a major-league player. His weak legs could no longer carry him to glory. He had played in 2,401 major-league games, had made 2,415 hits, scored 1,677 runs, batted in 1,500 runs, and stolen 200 bases. His magnificent fielding, his powerful bat, and his blazing inspiration to teammates had sparked the New York Yankees to twelve pennants. In World Series combat, he hit more home runs than any other player —18 in all.

In 1974, when Mickey Mantle had aged to 43, he finally completed the baseball mission which his father had dedicated him to since birth. It ended in a most glorious way. He was enshrined in Cooperstown's Hall of Fame, ever to be honored and remembered as one of baseball's immortals.

KING KELLY

"Once a King, Always a King"

Back in the late 1880's and early 1890's, the top baseball idol was the tall, powerfully built, mustachioed, handsome Irishman, Michael Joseph Kelly from Troy, New York. So glamorous and versatile was he that he became nationally known as the "King of Baseball."

King Kelly began playing baseball on the sandlots of Paterson, New Jersey, where he worked for three dollars a week. By twenty, he was playing semi-professional baseball, and by twenty-one, he was in the big leagues as a catcher and outfielder for the 1878 Cincinnati club. Whenever needed, he also played first base, second, third, and shortstop, too. He was almost a one-man baseball team.

Two years later, King Kelly, who had become the first big-league player to be followed on the streets by admiring fans and autograph seekers, moved on to the Chicago White Stockings of the National League, where he sparked Cap Anson's team to five pennants in six years. He was so ingenious, tricky, quick-thinking and smart on a ball field that he practically wrote the rules. Not only did the amazing King Kelly do everything possible for one player to perform, but he did many

things first in major-league play. He was the first player to circle the bases in less than 15 seconds, and so sensationally daring was his base-running and sliding to the bags that it led fans to create the slogan "Slide, Kelly, Slide!" which became a byword of the game.

After winning the 1886 batting crown with a lofty .388 average, fabulous King Kelly was sold to the Boston club in the National League for $10,000. He thereby became the first ballplayer to be sold for and to get "important money" for his incomparable skills. The Boston club had agreed to pay him $5,000 a year. Newspaper editorals were written about the $10,-000 Beauty"—the baseball hero who was earning the highest season's salary ever paid a professional player.

So joyous were the Boston baseball fans to have King Kelly play for their home-town team that they presented him with a gold-trimmed carriage drawn by a glistening white horse so he could ride to the ballpark in style. At times, frenzied admirers themselves would unhitch the horse and pull King Kelly's carriage through the streets, while others cheered and tossed flowers in his path. King Kelly also sparked the Boston team to pennants. In his 16 years in the majors, he played with eight pennant winners.

But if King Kelly was a unique hero for his matchless feats on a ball field, he was something special and unique off the playing field, too. In his time, he was a fashion plate beyond compare, the first baseball player to gain national fame as a best-dressed man. Always wearing the finest-tailored stylish clothes, an ultrafashionable Ascot around his neck, patent leather shoes on his feet, and a tall hat on his head, he was indeed a handsome sight.

King Kelly was paid high fees to model the latest fashions in stylish wear. Clothing manufacturers begged him to wear their garments to give them a special distinction. Fashion magazines featured stories about his attire, and throughout the land he was featured on billboards.

When he went on a tour of Europe, there, too, fashion experts praised the style, dash and flair of the distinctive clothes he wore, and before long, King Kelly was being acclaimed as the best-dressed man in the world. No hero in sports history ever came even close to King Kelly's fame as a clotheshorse.

He was 36 when he quit the major leagues as a player and went on the stage, so that he could continue living royally, be the graceful spender he was, and live up to his nickname of King. But only a year later, the Grim Reaper struck out mighty King Kelly—a victim of pneumonia at age 37.

For his true greatness as a big-league baseball hero he was given a place in Cooperstown's Hall of Fame with other immortals of the game. But into the hallowed shrine King Kelly carried with him a distinction possessed by no other: Only he was ever acknowledged as being the world's best-dressed man!

ROBERTO CLEMENTE
Latin Wonderman

A big-league player who can live like a baseball hero and depart from this world like a hero is truly a rare and glorious idol for the ages. Roberto Clemente was such a man.

His saga began in the town of Carolina, Puerto Rico, where he was born into a middle-class home. As a teen-ager, he became an outstanding high school athlete, playing varsity baseball, and starring in track, as a high-jumper, broad-jumper, and javelin thrower.

Although he had vague ideas of becoming an engineer, they disappeared when the owner of the Santurce Professional baseball club saw young Roberto engineer pitches out of a ballpark with a bat in hand during an amateur baseball game. Promptly, Roberto was hired as a professional baseball player, for a bonus of $500, and a munificent salary of $60 a month. He was 17 years old then.

Roberto was an immediate sensation as a hard-hitting outfielder. Before long, a big-league scout saw him play, and gave him a $10,000 bonus to sign a contract with the Brooklyn Dodgers. So, 19-year-old Clemente left Puerto Rico for Montreal to play for the Dodgers' top farm club and acquire some seasoning for the big leagues.

Somehow, the Brooklyn Dodgers allowed Roberto Clemente to slip away from them, because he was picked up by the Pittsburgh Pirates for a measly $4,000. He was 21 then.

Thus began the era of Roberto Clemente in the major leagues. During the eighteen years that he starred for the Pittsburgh Pirates, he not only became as magnificent a right fielder as ever played the game, but he also became one of the all-time hitting greats. Astonishing were his many feats with glove and bat.

His fielding magic was breathtaking. Nobody ever caught fly balls quite like Clemente in right field. He threw with such remarkable power that he collected 4,697 putouts for his fame. So wondrous were his fielding skills that the annual "Golden Glove Award" was bestowed upon him twelve times for being the outstanding outfielder in the majors.

At bat, the slat-lean, 71-inch, 175-pound Clemente was a slashing, free-swinging hitter. In 2,433 major-league games, with 9,454 times at bat, he made 3,000 safe hits, to become only the eleventh player in history for such a feat. He flavored his remarkable hitting with 1,416 runs scored, 1,305 runs batted-in, and 240 homers, accumulating a .317 lifetime batting average. And to add to his glory as one of baseball's all-time hitting marvels, Clemente captured four National League batting championships.

He was an exciting baseball hero, even though, ironically, for years he was unappreciated and unpublicized, simply because there were several other fabulous stars then on the major-league scene. But eventually, the entire baseball world came to acclaim him as an idol of pure gold.

Three times his super-playing sparked the Pittsburgh Pirates to pennants and World Series championships. He made the 1971 World Series a "Clemente Spectacular," for he outglittered all the other players in that classic with his brilliant fielding and devastating hitting. He made 12 hits in the seven games played to win the world championship for his team. In season and post-season diamond battle, Roberto Clemente was a baseball hero.

But there was yet more to him than that. He was the gentlest of players, and a wonderful human being. Despite his eminent status of being a $150,000-a-season star, he had concern for all and constantly helped others. Always he was the first to lend a hand and give advice to scared and struggling rookies.

Roberto Clemente was crowding 39, but still at the peak of his fame when he flew off in a plane on a mission of mercy on New Year's Eve, 1972. He was attempting to bring relief supplies, in medicine and food, to the victims of an earthquake in Managua, Nicaragua. It was a foggy rainy night, and the plane crashed and fell into the sea miles off the shores of San Juan, Puerto Rico. The waters swallowed Roberto Clemente, and his body was never found.

So he had lived and died a hero. For his last hurrah he was enshrined in the National Baseball Hall of Fame with all the other diamond greats. He was the first Latin-American baseball player to enter the hallowed shrine for his everlasting glory.

His supreme baseball talent made Roberto Clemente famous. But his humanity made him immortal.

BILLY SUNDAY
God's Outfielder

Born in 1862, and reared in an orphan asylum, William Ashley Sunday was twenty-one when he was plucked off the Iowa sandlots to play baseball in the big leagues as an outfielder for the old Chicago National League club. He made his big-league debut on May 22, 1883, and quickly set a baseball record for a rookie that still stands. He struck out the first fourteen times he came to bat.

As a swift, clever, sure-handed outfielder, however, he went on to fame. He was the first major-league player to circle the bases in less than thirteen seconds. Billy starred for ten seasons— for the Chicago White Stockings, the Pittsburgh Pirates, and the Philadelphia Phillies—and became one of the most popular and highest-paid players.

Off the field, Billy was a guy strictly for good times. His escapades were wild and many, and he could "bend an elbow" with the best. One night, while on a gay spree, he came upon a street-corner religious meeting. A group of men and women were singing gospel hymns. Billy Sunday listened for a while, and then, suddenly, he "got religion." He turned to his night companions and said, "Boys, I'm finished with this wild life. I'm going into the service of God. I've seen the Light!"

None of his teammates took him seriously. Several days later, when at the height of his fame, he startled the baseball world by quitting baseball to do religious work for the Young Men's Christian Association at a salary of $83 a month.

Billy Sunday became an evangelist: a rough-and-ready ripsnorting preacher of sin and salvation. In the frenzy of his preaching to sinners, he would thump his chest, tear off his coat, collar and tie, leap up on chairs, and fling himself on the floor in imitation of a ballplayer sliding in to home plate. Millions flocked to hear Billy Sunday deliver his vigorous message of sin and salvation. Billy Sunday became the most colorful and most famous evangelist in the world.

For thirty-five years, this ex-big-league outfielder preached the gospel of salvation as flaring headlines followed his wanderings. In the process of lambasting the devil and exhorting men and women to renounce their ungodly ways, Billy Sunday preached to more than a hundred million people. He converted at least a million of them in his campaigns. "I'm God's outfielder!" he told all who listened to him.

When his health began to fail, baseball-hero-turned-evangelist told his friends, "I'm on third base, waiting to slide home safely." In 1935, almost to the exact November day he had entered this world seventy-three years earlier, Billy Sunday left it, and "went home"—safe in his immortality.

To this day, the legend of the one-time baseball hero who quit the game to become "God's outfielder" is still vivid in memory. Books have been written, a motion picture has been filmed, and even an opera has been composed, based on the once-fabulous, incomparable Billy Sunday.

PETE GRAY

The One-Armed Outfielder

Perhaps the most amazing and unlikely baseball player of all time was Peter J. Wyshner, born in Nanticoke, Pennsylvania. He was the only one-armed man ever to play in the major leagues. How that came to pass is an unbelievable tale of courage and determination in a struggle to achieve the impossible.

Tragedy came early to Petey. He was

only six years old when he lost his right arm, just below the shoulder. He had been standing on the running board of a truck when it pulled out suddenly, hurling him against an embankment and bouncing him back. He thrust out his right arm, which went into the open spokes of a wheel. Amputation was necessary to save the boy's life.

But as the boy grew older, his handicap did not deter him from playing baseball. By the time Petey was a teenager, he had become so skillful a player that people throughout that coal-mining country were spreading the news: "You should see that one-armed youngster from Nanticoke play baseball. You won't believe it."

Local fame wasn't enough for one-armed Petey, however. He was consumed with only one desire, to become a big-league ballplayer. He could field

and catch a baseball with his one arm, and hit it with surprising ease and power. When he caught a ball, he would stick the glove under the stub of his right arm and throw the ball back, all in the same smooth motion. It seemed like an optical illusion.

Finally, in 1942, when he was 24 years old, he got his chance to play in organized baseball. He adopted the name of his brother who was boxing professionally under the name of Whitey Gray, and as Peter Gray he became a minor-league baseball player. The Three Rivers club of the Canadian-American League hired him as an outfielder. Though rookie Pete Gray broke his collarbone early in his first season in the minors, he wound up with the best batting average in the league— .381 in 42 games played.

From there, one-armed outfielder Gray moved on to Memphis, where he batted .289 in 126 games played. Then came his most glorious season as a minor-league player. He did it all in the Southern League for the Memphis team when he fielded magnificently as an outfield fly hawk, collected 119 safe hits for a total of 221 bases, drove in 60 runs, and wound up with a .333 batting average. He also hit five home runs, and stole 68 bases.

Pete Gray's astonishing performance as a minor-league wonder finally earned him his chance in the big leagues. In 1945, the old St. Louis Browns bought him from Memphis for $20,000.

And so, a miracle happened. A one-armed outfielder came to play in the major leagues. The Browns paid Pete Gray a season's salary of $5,500. He was twenty-eight years old then.

Pete Gray became a tremendous

gate attraction as a major-league base-ball hero. Thousands flocked to the ballpark to see the one-armed wonder perform his magical catches. In that memorable 1945 season, no other out-fielder could rouse a crowd to excitment the way Pete Gray did.

He starred in 77 major-league games, and batted .200-plus for his everlasting fame as the only one-armed outfielder ever to play in the big leagues.

The amazing Pete Gray played only that one season for the St. Louis Browns, never again to bask in the spotlight of baseball competition. After that year, the Browns gave him another $1,500 for his efforts on the diamond, and he went home to Nanticoke to re-live his memories.

While Pete Gray didn't set the base-ball world on fire with his modest glories, he did make an impossible dream come true, and fulfilled his life's desire to play in the big time, despite the disheartening handicap of being minus one arm. That was quite a feat to accomplish. It made courageous Pete Gray a unique hero in baseball history.

THE WANER BOYS
Big Poison and Little Poison

On April 16, the opening day of the 1903 baseball season, a boy was born on a ranch in Hurrah, Oklahoma. He was named Paul Glee Waner. On March 16, 1906, he was joined by his newly born brother, Lloyd James Waner. The two Waner Boys grew up to become unique baseball heroes, and playing side by side for the same major-league team, they staged the most in-credible brother act in all baseball his-tory.

Since their father once had been a professional baseball player, the Waner brothers were exposed to baseball as soon as each could walk. Because money for proper baseball gear was scarce in the Waner household, Paul and Lloyd improvised nicely in their early boyhood for their baseball play-ing. They used a hoe handle for a bat, and a corncob for a ball, after soaking it in a pail of water to make it tough and hard to withstand their battering. The two brothers spent countless hours playing baseball whenever each had finished with his daily chores, milking seventeen cows each morning.

Paul was the first of the Waner Boys to become a professional baseball player. For three years he had been a student at State Teachers College at Ada, Oklahoma, playing amateur and semi-pro baseball in that territory while

standing minor-league player for three seasons. Curiously, Lloyd Waner was hardly any bigger than his older brother, Paul, for he, too, stood only 68 inches tall and weighed less than 150 pounds. Unlike his brother, he was a right-hander.

Paul Waner's debut as a big-league rookie was phenomenal. Not only was he spectacular as a fleet-footed, sure-handed fly hawk in right field, but his hitting was astonishing, too. In the 144 games he played, he slashed out 180 hits, achieved six hits in six times at bat in one game, and wound up with a .336 batting average.

Rookie Paul Waner still wasn't fully satisfied playing for the Pittsburgh Pirates without his younger brother by his side, so he persuaded the Pirates' club owner to hire Lloyd as an out-fielder, which the owner did. The 1927 season began with rookie Lloyd Waner in center field for the Pirates, and older brother Paul in right field for his sopho-more year in the big leagues. That sea-son, the Waner Boys staged an act of playing greatness unique in baseball history.

Rookie Lloyd set an all-time fresh-man record for safe hits in one season, 223, and wound up with a final batting average of .355 for his glory. Older brother Paul was even more incredible. He led the league in safe hits with 237, and 131 runs batted in. He won the batting championship with a lofty .380 average, and won the Most Valuable Player honors. That season the amaz-ing playing of the Waner Brothers sparked the Pirates to a pennant. And from that memorable year on, Paul was known as "Big Poison," while his kid

expecting to become a teacher, when a baseball scout spotted him and signed him for the San Francisco Seals of the Pacific Coast League. Paul Waner was then 20 years old, and not too impres-sive-looking as an outfielder for minor-league fame. He stood only 68 inches tall, and barely weighed 135 pounds.

Nevertheless, he became a sensation as a minor-league baseball hero. In the three seasons he starred for the Seals, he never hit under .360; and once, he hit over .400 for his fame. Those were his credentials for the Pittsburgh Pirates to shell out $100,000 to buy him and bring him to the big leagues. But before the 23-year-old little lefty went off in pursuit of major-league glory, he per-suaded the San Francisco Seals to hire his 20-year-old kid brother Lloyd as an outfielder. Lloyd also became an out-brother Lloyd was known as "Little Poison."

For fifteen years, playing side by side in the Pirates' outfield, they terrorized all opposing pitchers as no brothers ever did in big-league history. Both Waner boys, each towering no more than 68 inches tall in all their majesty, were complete ballplayers. They could field, throw, steal bases, hit, and beat opponents in many ways.

Ten times in his first twelve seasons in the majors, Lloyd hit over .300, and three times he batted over .350 a season. Four times he collected more than 200 hits a season.

Older brother Paul was even more outstanding as a super-batsman. Fourteen times he hit over .300—twelve times in a row. Six times he batted over .360 and won the National League batting championship three times. Strangely, at the peak of his batting fame, Paul was so nearsighted that he barely saw the outfield fences when at bat.

During all their years of glory, the Waner Boys were completely unlike each other. Lloyd was shy and retiring, meticulous in his clean-living habits. He never sought evening amusements, and religiously obeyed training rules and curfew hours to keep in perfect playing condition.

But older brother Paul was an outgoing gay blade who pursued the good life to the hilt. He ignored training rules and curfew hours in a nightly prowl for fun and good times. Often, he imbibed to excess, but it never hindered his phenomenal playing.

Once, before an important game, the Pittsburgh manager found a half-filled whiskey bottle in the Pirates' locker room. Angrily, he confronted Paul Waner, snapping at him: "Is this half-filled whiskey bottle yours?"

"Nope, skipper," calmly and nonchalantly replied little Paul. "If it were mine, it would be empty by now!" The manager never again bothered Paul Waner about his drinking pleasures.

So glamorous and popular did the Waner Boys become that they often toured the country with a vaudeville show out of season, Paul playing the saxophone and Lloyd the violin.

"Little Poison" lasted 19 seasons in the big leagues, starring for three teams. He was 39 when he left the majors with 2,459 hits, 1,201 runs scored, and a .316 lifetime batting average.

"Big Poison" lasted 21 years in the big leagues, playing for four teams. He was past 42 when he left the majors with an awesome record for his greatness. In the 2,549 games he had played in, little Paul had slashed out 3,152 hits, scored 1,628 runs, batted in 1,309 runs, and compiled a .333 lifetime batting average.

Between them, the amazing Waner Boys had collected an unbelievable total of 5,611 major-league hits—a record unapproached by any other set of brothers.

Today, the fabulous Waner Boys are still unique in their glory as never-to-be-forgotten heroes. For Paul and Lloyd Waner are the only two brothers enshrined in baseball's Hall of Fame.

HENRY ["Hank"] AARON

Just Plain Old Hank

Back in the 1954 baseball season, when an unknown, shy 20-year-old rookie named Hank Aaron came to bat for the first time in a major-league game, the rival catcher looked him over and mockingly commented, "Hey, kid, you're holding your bat wrong. You ought to hold it so you can read the label on it."

"I didn't come here to read—I came to hit," snapped back the rookie. Then he belted the first pitch thrown to him for a safe hit.

On April 8, 1974, forty-year-old outfielder Hank Aaron, playing in his twenty-first major-league season, hit his 715th big-league home run, and went into the record books as the top home-run slugger of all time. He also had by that time a flock of superstar statistics —more than 3,500 safe hits, including 584 doubles and 96 triples, worth an impressive 2,133 runs-batted-in, and almost 2,000 runs scored.

Hank Aaron had come a long way from the sandlots of Mobile, Alabama, on the road to greatness.

Humble and doubtful was his beginning as a professional baseball player. Poor, shy and retiring, the black youngster did not mix easily with the other neighborhood boys in their athletic games, even though he was much in de-

mand. A studious lad, he preferred reading books at the library. At Central High School he did not play baseball— the school didn't have a baseball team. But he often played on the sandlots of Mobile. At 15, he was spotted by a baseball scout while playing for a semi-pro team for three dollars a game.

When he was only 16, the Indianapolis Clowns of the Negro American League offered Hank Aaron a contract for $200 a month to play for their team. No sooner had he graduated from high school than he left Mobile to join them, carrying two dollars in his pocket, two pairs of pants in a cheap cardboard suitcase, and some sandwiches his mother had made to sustain him on the long train ride.

Though young Aaron had an unorthodox batting style (he held his bat cross-handed, placing his left hand above his right hand, a clumsy grip for a right-handed hitter), he began hitting so impressively that big-league scouts began following the Indianapolis team just to watch Hank Aaron play. The Boston Braves outbid all the other teams for Hank Aaron's baseball contract, then farmed him out for two years to the minors. When the 1954 season began, Hank Aaron became their regular right fielder. He was only twenty then.

In Milwaukee, where the Boston Braves had moved their franchise, rookie Hank Aaron drew little attention. He hit only 13 home runs and batted only .280, but the following season, when he hit 27 home runs and batted .314, many began to believe that he was on his way to superstardom. In his third year, Hank Aaron won the first of his two batting titles, and his homer production continued to climb.

As the seasons went by, magnificent right fielder Hank Aaron achieved astonishing feats. Eight times he led the National League in total bases, and four times in homers and runs-batted-in. Only he, in National League history, hit 40 or more homers a season seven times. And only he, in all major-league history, ever hit 20 or more homers a season seventeen times in a row. No pitcher seemed immune to the devastation in Hank Aaron's bat.

In the outfield, he was an effortless performer with such fly-hawk efficiency that four times he won the coveted "Gold Glove" award bestowed annually upon the outstanding outfielder. The most daring base-runners rarely took chances on his powerful throwing arm to steal an extra base. Curiously, Hank Aaron himself was a smart and daring base-stealer. He stole nearly 300 bases for his fame.

Although Hank Aaron became one of the superstars, as well as the highest-paid baseball player of all time (a salary of $200,000 a season), he remained the most modest and unpretentious ballplayer in the game. He still referred to himself as "just plain old Hank."

When the Braves again moved their franchise in 1966, this time to Atlanta, their superstar Hank Aaron was so widely idolized that the fans of the South paid tribute to him at a special "Hank Aaron Day" at the ballpark. It was the first such event for a black man in the history of Southern sports.

In 1974, "just plain old Hank," now 40 years old, was still playing, enriching his fame as the greatest home run hitter—a fabulous baseball hero bound for diamond immortality.

Which wasn't bad for the once shy poor kid who had left Mobile twenty-four years earlier with two dollars and two pairs of pants in a cheap cardboard suitcase to become a professional baseball player.

MARVELS ON THE INFIELD

ADRIAN ["Cap"] ANSON
The Daddy of All First Basemen

No man ever played big-league baseball as many years as Adrian C. ("Cap") Anson of Marshalltown, Iowa. One of the game's first outstanding stars, his active career spanned three generations of baseball players. He played for twenty-seven years.

Standing 6 feet, 2 inches tall and weighing 220 pounds, Cap Anson became the first great first baseman of note. He is considered the "daddy" of them all.

A first-base guardian of matchless fielding skill for the Chicago White Stockings of the National League, he was also one of the best hitters in the history of the sport. A right-handed batter, he became the first player to make 3,000 hits. For twenty consecutive seasons he never hit below .300, and twice he batted above the .400 mark. He won five batting championships, collected a lifetime total of 3,524 hits, and wound up with a batting average of .339.

At the height of his career, Cap Anson's name was synonymous with

baseball. A ballplayer of integrity, sobriety, personal purity, and dignity, he had a tremendous influence on the game.

But the daddy of all first basemen became more than an incomparable performer. He became the most successful player-manager big-league baseball ever had. In his thirteen years as playing skipper of the National League Chicago club, he piloted his team to five pennants and four second-place finishes. No other player-manager ever matched his record.

The foremost baseball strategist of his time, Cap Anson was a stickler for rigid physical conditioning for himself and his players. He hounded them to keep trim and fit, to watch their diet, and to keep regular sleeping hours. He was, indeed, an example for all ballplayers.

The start of each baseball season was always a trying time for Cap Anson.

Invariably, his players would report for action hog-fat and woefully out of condition after a winter of loafing and high living.

But in 1886, Cap Anson decided to do something radically different. Several weeks before the start of that baseball season, he ordered his players to report for work. When the puzzled players showed up, Cap Anson took them to a training camp he had set up in Hot Springs, Arkansas. There he put them through daily rigorous training sessions to get them into good physical shape. Although most of the men complained and grumbled, nevertheless, when the baseball campaign began, the Chicago players were in such fine physical condition that they breezed their way to the pennant.

When other baseball managers saw what Cap Anson had accomplished, they set up pre-season training camps of their own. Thus started spring training for all major-league players.

In 1897, when Cap Anson was forty-five years old, he starred in his final season in the big leagues.

Born in April, 1852, he died in April, 1922, a baseball idol to the end. And his feats as a first baseman properly warranted his election to baseball's Hall of Fame.

If all else should be forgotten of him as an outstanding ballplayer, a matchless manager, and an incomparable pacemaker who set a standard for all major-league players, what Cap Anson originated for the good of the national pastime will never be forgotten—spring training!

LOU GEHRIG

The Iron Horse

Born and bred in New York City, the son of German immigrant parents, Henry Louis Gehrig grew up into a strong, magnificently built teen-ager who became an outstanding schoolboy athlete. When he entered Columbia University, he gained fame as a football and baseball star. His mother, who was employed there as a cook, hoped that he would become an architect. However, all he ever created for his mother's happiness was a baseball legend.

Curiously, it was his father who indirectly forced him into becoming a professional baseball player. When Lou's father became seriously ill and needed an operation, there was no money in the family budget for doctors and hospital expenses, so young Gehrig quickly capitalized on his baseball skills. He accepted an offer from a scout to sign a contract with the New York Yankees for $1,500 in cash, as a bonus. Then he dropped out of college to play in the minor leagues and gain some pro experience until the Yankees would need him.

Gehrig was 22 when he became a big-league rookie. He sat on the bench until one day in June of the 1925 season when he finally broke into the Yankees' lineup as a first baseman. It happened because the team's veteran first

baseman couldn't play, due to a severe headache. For Lou Gehrig it was the beginning of a fantastic saga of durability, consistency, longevity, and glory. He remained at first base for the Yankees during the next fourteen seasons, comprising 5,082 playing days, until he had played a total of 2,130 major-league games. It was a record that will never be broken nor even equaled.

To create that unbelievable endurance feat, strong and powerful Lou Gehrig, nicknamed "The Iron Horse," played in every one of the 2,130 consecutive games, even though he was beaned three times, had fingers broken ten times, suffered fractured toes, torn muscles, a wrenched shoulder, a back injury, chipped elbows, and the pain of several lumbago attacks. Yet, in every contest of that incredibly long playing period he played with all the enthusiasm of a kid breaking into the big leagues.

During that streak of 2,130 consecutive games, "The Iron Horse" performed other astonishing feats. He became the first player in the 20th century to hit four consecutive home runs in a nine-inning game. Only he in major-league history ever hit 23 grand slam home runs. For thirteen years in a row he drove in 100 runs, topping 150 RBI's seven times and setting the American League record of 184 runs-batted-in during the 1931 season. For twelve seasons in a row, he hit over .300, and he made 1,190 extra base hits, 493 of them home runs. He batted in 1,991 runs, scored 1,888 runs, and walked 1,510 times. He won the coveted "Triple Crown" of the majors, the Most Valuable Player award, made 2,721 safe hits for a lifetime batting average of .340. His magnificent playing helped the Yankees win seven pennants and six World Series championships.

Though he had begun in the big leagues as a clumsy, poor-fielding first baseman, "Larrupin' Lou," as he also came to be known, overcame his faults through perseverance, patience, tireless practice and hard work, and blossomed out into as smooth and skillful a first baseman as ever lived.

More than all this, though he never was flamboyant nor spectacular, and never sought the headlines, clean-living Gehrig of exemplary habits became an idolized and inspirational hero to millions of boys throughout America.

Ironically, "The Iron Horse," the strongest and most durable big-league player of his time, became a victim of a cruel fate. When Gehrig was 36, and still in his prime, he was felled by a mysterious disease that robbed him of his strength, power and coordination. Puzzled doctors diagnosed his illness as amyotrophic lateral sclerosis, a form of paralysis affecting the spinal cord. It is now referred to as "Gehrig's disease."

On a May afternoon in that 1939 season he benched himself as the Yankees' first baseman because he could no longer help his team. He wept when it happened, and he never played again.

On a July 4th afternoon of that memorable season more than 75,000 loyal fans flocked into the vast Yankees' ballpark to pay homage to Lou Gehrig and bid him farewell. Although the fabled "Iron Horse" knew that he was dying, he stood at home plate and told the huge hushed throng:

"Fans, they tell me I've been given a bad break. But I've got wonderful parents, a wife who loves me, and I've played baseball with the greatest teammates a ballplayer ever could hope for. I've had my share of good things in life. With all the good I've had, today, I consider myself to be the luckiest man on the face of the earth."

Less than two years later, Lou Gehrig was dead at 38. A nation mourned for him. Baseball's Hall of Fame immortalized him. His locker in the Yankees' clubhouse was turned into a shrine. No Yankee player ever again wore Gehrig's famed number 4 on a baseball uniform. Hollywood filmed a motion picture of his life, appropriately entitled "The Pride of the Yankees." And near the Yankees' ballpark, where for fifteen years he had made imperishable history, a street was named in his honor—Lou Gehrig Plaza.

GEORGE SISLER
"Gorgeous George"

George Sisler undoubtedly was the most graceful fielding first baseman of all time. He also registered a .340 batting average for 16 years in the majors, including two seasons in which he went over .400. One year he laced 257 hits—more hits in a single season than anyone in the game's history.

Yet, astonishingly, he broke into the big leagues as a left-handed pitcher— and a very good one, good enough to best the immortal Walter Johnson when that worthy was at the top of his form.

Sisler was born in Manchester, Ohio, in 1893, and pitched for an Akron high school, and later, at the University of Michigan. He was practically unbeatable, and when he was graduated with a degree in engineering, he signed with the old St. Louis Browns. It was something of a favor to his college coach, the great Branch Rickey, who had become a major-league manager and was then piloting that team in the American League.

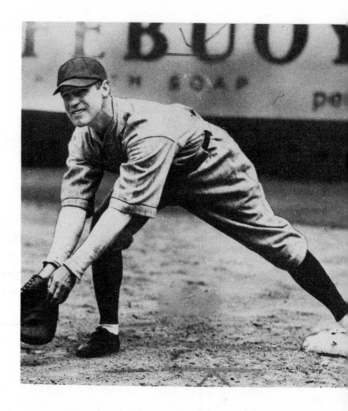

Upon joining the Browns, Sisler was utilized as a pitcher (he won four games as a raw rookie, including the victory over Johnson), outfielder, and first baseman. But it soon became apparent that his bat was too valuable not to have a definite place in the lineup, so he became the regular first-sacker. It was a job he held for the rest of his major-league career.

His reflexes and native intelligence made him a peerless first baseman, just as they made him one of the smartest hitters ever to play. Once, in a close game at Boston's Fenway Park, the Red Sox had men on first and third with no outs when the batter flied to left field. The outfielder, conceding the run, made a surprise throw to Sisler at first, beating the runner returning to first for a double play. Without an instant's hesitation or lost motion, Sisler rifled the ball to the catcher who tagged the runner coming in from third. It was a remarkable triple play.

Another time, Sisler fielded a routine grounder behind first and lofted the ball to the bag where the approaching pitcher would cover. The pitcher was late and, realizing that, Sisler raced over, caught his own throw—and retired the hitter.

But it was at the plate that Sisler made his most phenomenal contributions. By his third year with the Browns, he was a .353 hitter, and he followed in the next six years with these marks: .341, .352, .352, .407, .371, and .420. Only one man in American League history, Nap Lajoie, back in 1901, ever hit higher than that last figure. Lajoie hit .422. During the 1922 season, he batted safely in 41 consecutive games for a league record which stood for 19 years until Hall-of-Famer Joe DiMaggio broke it. At the end of that glorious season, he won the American League's first Most Valuable Player award.

On the heels of that fabulous year, however, when "Gorgeous George" was 29 and at the height of his fame, tragedy struck. He was stricken with acute sinusitis. Its affected his optic nerves and left him with double vision. Troubled Sisler was out of baseball for a whole year while doctors tried to save him from a creeping blindness. He won the grim battle for his eyesight with tenacity and courage, and returned to the big leagues.

George Sisler played again for eight more years, and though his marvelous reflexes and keen eyesight were not as they had been before his illness, he was still the game's most magnificent first baseman. For three seasons he was the playing manager of the St. Louis Browns, and then he starred for the Boston Braves of the National League until he was 37. He still was the game's most remarkable batter. He always hit over .300. Twice he batted over .340, and three times he collected more than 200 hits a season. He completed his dazzling career with 2,812 hits in 2,055 games played, and a lifetime batting average of .340, compiled after 8,267 times at bat. But for his eye trouble, George Sisler might have outstripped all players as the top hitter of all time.

When his big-league glory days were done, he was, of course, a natural for the Hall of Fame, and he was suitably enshrined there.

In time, George Sisler attained a unique distinction to add to his pride and happiness as a legendary hero. He became the only Hall of Fame immortal to send two sons to follow in his footsteps—Dick, who became a star first baseman, and David, who pitched creditably for teams in both major leagues.

EDWARD ["Big Ed"] DELAHANTY

The Greatest Enigma

In the long and dusty records of big-league baseball, only seven players have hit four home runs in a nine-inning game. The second player to achieve that incredible slugging feat was the fabled "Big Ed" Delahanty. He did it on July 13, 1896. But that was only one of the ferocious slugging feats of a ballplayer who was the equal of any right-handed batter to swing a bat.

There is one glorious distinction which Big Ed Delahanty still holds: he alone led both present major leagues in batting. He accomplished that by hitting .408 for the Philadelphia Phillies in 1899, to win the National League batting championship, and by hitting .376 for the Washington Senators in 1902, to win the American League batting crown.

Besides those feats of batting prominence, Big Ed once cracked out ten hits in succession over a two-game period, and on two occasions he made six hits in six times at bat. Another time he hit four doubles in a game; and seven times he batted better than .370, twice over the .400 level. He left a 16-year major-league batting average of .346.

Born in Cleveland, Ohio, in 1867, son of Irish immigrant parents who also produced four other sons to play big-

league baseball, Edward James was the foremost of the Delahanty baseball clan. He became a major-leaguer when he was 21, and quickly became the most glamorous baseball player of his time. He came into his own as a first baseman, and as an outstanding outfielder, too. But it was his superb hitting that set him apart from all other baseball greats of his era.

Big Ed's specialty was hitting wild pitches. With a long and heavy bat in his powerful hands, he would take delight belting bad pitches for safe hits. No wonder he collected 2,593 hits for his fame! In that ancient era of the dead ball, only mighty Big Ed hit as many as 100 home runs.

Despite his awesome status, Delahanty took his career lightly. He did little training, defied discipline, and lived merrily. It led to his end as a major-league wonder, and his exit from the game created the greatest enigma in baseball lore.

Fabulous Ed Delahanty played his last game for the Washington Senators in his home town of Cleveland on June 25, 1903. Before the game ended, that magnificent roughneck, still in his prime and batting .338, got into an argument with his manager that caused him to go haywire. With his Irish temper flared to a boiling point, he suddenly left the ballpark and boarded a train bound for an unknown destination. On the speeding train, Big Ed created such a wild disturbance that night, that when it stopped briefly at Fort Erie, Ontario, at the Canadian end of the International Bridge, he was kicked off the train.

In a wild rage, Delahanty stumbled off into the darkness—and was never again seen alive. Days later, after a frantic search, the mangled body of the famous ballplayer was found pinned against a wharf some twenty miles from Niagara Falls. His strange demise was never fully explained. Many believed that he had fallen off the bridge and drowned in the Niagara River. Others wondered if he had been the victim of foul play. Amid much speculation, no one really knew the answer.

He was only 36 when he came to his tragic end. It was ironic that the hero who gave the baseball world its most unbelievable batting feat also gave it its strangest mystery.

Big Ed Delahanty will never be forgotten, however, for he is now enshrined in the Cooperstown Hall of Fame as an immortal of baseball.

JIMMY FOXX

"The Beast"

One of the most feared of the baseball sluggers was mighty Jimmy Foxx, who, during one stretch of his magnificent 21-year major-league career, never hit fewer than 33 homers a season for twelve consecutive years—a record never equaled. Also, five times he surpassed 40 home runs a season.

The 5-foot-11-inch, 190-pound Foxx had such strength and power, and

ball. The puzzled and annoyed catcher thereupon walked to the mound and asked "What do you want to throw to him?" The pitcher shrugged and replied, "Nothing! Maybe he'll get tired and walk away." When the ball finally was delivered, Foxx hit it into the topmost (third) deck of Yankee Stadium, a distant spot that never had been reached before by any other home-run slugger, and unequaled afterward.

The lengths of his home runs were a chief topic of discussion. Foxx always maintained that his longest one was hit during an exhibition game in Tokyo's Meiji Stadium. It sailed more than 600 feet from home plate.

James Emory Foxx was a brawny, muscular farm boy from Sudlersville, Maryland, when, in 1925, he came to the major leagues as a catcher for the Philadelphia Athletics. He was only 17 years old. But wise manager Connie Mack turned him into a first baseman, and Jimmy blossomed into one of the finest first-sackers of them all. With his superb fielding and thundering bat, he sparked the Athletics to three consecutive pennants. Three times he was acclaimed Most Valuable Player of the American League.

As the seasons passed, "The Beast" (also nicknamed "Double-X") not only whammed baseballs as hard and as far as any man who ever lived, but he also revealed himself as one of the game's most versatile performers. The fabulous slugger, who began as a major-league catcher, also played third base, the outfield, and finished his career as a pitcher. Once, he also won the majors' most coveted prize for his versatility—the Triple Crown.

He starred for four different teams,

looked so menacing, that rival pitchers nicknamed him "The Beast." And with good reason. He lambasted them so often and with such consistency that he collected 2,543 safe hits in 2,317 games, and produced a .325 lifetime batting average in addition to his home-run figures. In the 1932 season, although he was sidelined for almost a month because of an injury, he finished with 58 home runs. He hit, all told, 534 home runs for his major-league fame.

One way rival pitchers got rid of "The Beast" when he was at bat was by walking him. He drew a total of 1,458 bases on balls. In one nine-inning game, he was walked six consecutive times (a record that still stands). In one important game, Foxx was batting against Hall-of-Fame pitcher Lefty Gomez of the New York Yankees, and the count went to three-and-two. With the game in the balance, the catcher signaled sign after sign, but the famous hurler just stood on the mound, not throwing the in both major leagues, until he hung up his spikes as a player at the age of 38. For a while he managed in the minors, then died tragically in 1967 at the age of sixty.

By then, there was no doubt that the legendary Beast would be remembered as one of the outstanding heroes of the game. Jimmy Foxx had a place in the Hall of Fame at Cooperstown.

ROGERS ["Rajah"] HORNSBY

From Weakling to Superman

Late in the 1915 season, there came to the big leagues a curious-looking 19-year-old rookie. He was sporting a badger haircut, shabby clothes, carried a carpetbag with all his worldly possessions in it, and his entire fortune was in his pocket—three dollars. He stood almost six feet tall, and barely weighed 135 pounds. He was a nobody from Winters, Texas, who had been bought by the St. Louis Cardinals from a bush-league baseball team for $200 as a possible infielder prospect. When the Cardinals' club owner saw the skinny rookie for the first time, he changed his mind and refused to pay him the ninety-dollar-a-month salary promised. Club owner and rookie finally settled for a season's salary of sixty dollars a month.

So began the major-league career of Rogers Hornsby, the greatest right-handed hitter in the game's history.

Rookie Hornsby's big-league debut was mediocre. He appeared in 18 games, came to bat 57 times, and collected only 14 hits. When his freshman season was over, the Cardinals' manager advised him kindly: "Kid, go home and fatten up over the winter, if you want to last in this game." When Rogers Hornsby returned for his second season, he had "fattened up" to become a strong 170-pounder who could swing a bat with authority. That season he played in 139 games, made 155 hits, and wound up with a .313 batting average. Over the following twenty-one seasons, Rogers Hornsby not only established himself as one of the foremost second basemen, but also as an incomparable hero for the ages.

For him there were no detours on the glory road. The game became his way of life. He lived, breathed and slept baseball. He watched his diet, slept at least ten hours a day, didn't smoke, drink or revel with his teammates, and during baseball seasons didn't even go to the movies or read much for fear of straining his eyes. His fanaticism to keep in perfect playing condition rewarded him well—he not only became as magnificent a second basemen as ever lived, but also a batting wonder beyond compare.

For 22 seasons, he hit better than .300; and three times, higher than .400! The ultimate batting feat of the many he performed was engraved into history in 1924 as a unique accomplishment. In that memorable season, the mighty "Rajah," as he came to be known, played in 143 major-league games, was at bat 536 times, and hit safely in all but 22 games. He made 227 hits, to wind up with a fantastic .424 batting average—the highest one-season mark in all modern major-league history.

But even more unbelievable was the Rajah's hitting spree that once stretched across a six-year span, from 1920 to 1925, inclusive. It was the most devastating batting to be achieved by a major-league player. He started with a .370 batting average for the 1920 season. Then he went on to compile, in a row, season-batting-averages of .397, .401, .384, .424, and .403! During that rampage, he came to bat 2,679 times, and hit safely 1,078 times, for a six-year batting average of .402!

As the greatest right-handed hitter, Rogers Hornsby won seven National League batting championships—six of them in a row. Twice he was honored as the Most Valuable Player of his league. When he became the playing manager of the St. Louis Cardinals, he proved to be a brilliant leader of ballplayers, for in 1926, he piloted the Cardinals to their first pennant and World Series championship. Three years later, when he became the playing manager of the Chicago Cubs, he again piloted his team to a pennant.

Rogers Hornsby glittered in the big leagues until he was 42 years old. By then, his credentials for admittance to baseball's Hall of Fame were solid. He had played in 2,192 major-league games, had come to bat 8,173 times, had scored 1,579 runs, batted in 1,579, and made 2,930 hits to wind up with the second highest lifetime batting average in history—a lofty .358!

As long as big-league baseball is played, Rogers Hornsby will be remembered as the outstanding right-handed hitter in the game's history.

JACKIE ROBINSON

Trailblazing Champ

Jackie Robinson came to the big leagues late and left early. During his brief stay, he not only revolutionized the game, but gave America's national pastime a new meaning. He was the most exciting and competitive player ever known, a vital "first" for baseball history.

Born into a broken home, in a share-cropper's shabby cabin on a Southern plantation in Cairo, Georgia, John Roosevelt Robinson knew poverty and humiliation from the beginning of his life. Before he was eight years old, his mother, a domestic, packed up her brood of five children and went off to California. There Jackie lived his early boyhood, and grew up into a restless and tough youngster, running with street gangs in search of mischief and trouble.

As he grew older, though, he rode his unusual and varied athletic skills into schoolboy stardom, and eventually wound up on the right road as a student at the University of California at Los Angeles, where he gained widespread fame as an all-around athlete. He was an outstanding running halfback in college football, an All-America forward in basketball, a record-breaking star in track, an extraordinary boxer, and he played baseball with a special brilliance.

Then came World War II, and Jackie Robinson was commissioned an infantry lieutenant in the service of his country. Years after the conflict was over, in 1947, Jackie Robinson suddenly emerged from nowhere to play for the Brooklyn Dodgers. He was regarded as a rookie freak—because he was 28 years old, and he was black. He was the first black man to play in the major leagues. That proud rookie had come to organized baseball grimly determined to shatter its racial barrier for all time. As a ballplayer with a mission and a cause to fight for, he did it with guts, courage, fearless daring, and magnificent diamond skills, unequalled by any other rookie in big-league history.

In the beginning, it was a brutal ordeal for trailblazer Robinson. The pressures on him were almost unbearable. He became the most abused, most humiliated rookie in baseball history. He took a merciless "riding" from malicious rival players and bigoted fans. Cruel racial taunts were hurled at him constantly, and he had to endure outrageous vituperation at every turn. His life was often threatened if he continued playing in the majors, and some teams threatened to refuse to play against the Dodgers if Jackie Robinson was in their lineup. Even some of his own teammates complained about playing with the black rookie in their midst.

But in silent dignity and with great pride, rookie infielder Robinson continued to play with matchless skills, performing spectacular feats. He knew all too well that he not only had to be as good as the best, but even better. In his first big-league season, he played in 151 games, performing so brilliantly that he was acclaimed "Rookie of the Year." He also sparked the Brooklyn Dodgers to the National League pennant.

As the seasons went by, Jackie Robinson not only became as qualified a second baseman as any other, but he also became one of baseball's most idolized heroes. There never was another player who could beat a rival team in as many different ways as incredible Jackie. Not only was he the most electrifying second baseman around, but whenever needed, he also performed as a first baseman, shortstop, third baseman, or outfielder. Wherever he played, he excelled.

A natural firebrand, he was the most daring base-stealer of his time. His cunning unsettled all enemy pitchers and defenses. Only Jackie Robinson ever stole home 19 times in big-league play.

He constantly performed unusual feats to stay at the top. One season he would win the league's batting championship with a .342 mark, another season he would lead the loop in stolen bases, and still another season he would wind up the leader in double plays, or finish a season acclaimed as the league's Most Valuable Player.

During his brief ten-year stay in the major leagues, he played in 1,382 games and made 1,518 safe hits for a .311 lifetime batting average. But so magnificent was his talent with glove and bat that he sparked the Brooklyn Dodgers to six pennants.

Though he was 38 and still one of the highest-paid stars, he lost interest in the game when the Dodgers traded him to the New York Giants, and he promptly quit as a player. But that was not yet the end of the Jackie Robinson legend. Crowding 44, he again made baseball history with an astonishing "first" achievement: He became the first black player to be enshrined in the Cooperstown Hall of Fame.

Always it will be remembered that it was Jackie Robinson who gave America's national pastime a greater meaning and glory as a game for all ballplayers with exceptional skills, regardless of color or race.

NAPOLEON LAJOIE

The Most Graceful Player

In baseball's Hall of Fame, Napoleon Lajoie holds a unique distinction: He is the only player on the roster singled out for his grace. There was simply no one who ever fielded, threw, and batted with the grace of the legendary Frenchman, the greatest of all second basemen.

Lajoie was born in Woonsocket, Rhode Island. When he was still a boy, he was already doing a man's work to help support his widowed mother and her brood of seven children. Only on Sundays could he find the time to play some sandlot baseball.

The big, dark, handsome Lajoie was driving a hack for a livery stable in 1896 when he was plucked from obscurity to play professional baseball with the Fall River club of the New England League. He was twenty-one years old. When he learned that he would be paid as much as $100 a month, he gleefully exclaimed, "By Gar! From now on, Napoleon will play only baseball!" And how he played it!

Even before completing his first season as a professional, he crashed the big leagues. The Philadelphia Phillies bought him for $1,500. Lajoie remained a star second baseman in the majors for twenty-one years, and his exploits established him as the No. 1 second baseman of all time.

No other keystone guardian ever topped his skill as a fielder and batter, and no other ballplayer ever matched his incomparable grace on a ball field. Every move of his was a picture of effortless rhythm. He scooped up the hardest infield drives with unbelievable assurance and ease.

In 1901, when the National League Philadelphia club refused to pay him a salary of $2,500 a season, Lajoie jumped to the newly organized American League to play for the Philadelphia Athletics. In his first season in that circuit, the 6-foot-1 Frenchman set such a furious pace that it hasn't been matched by an American Leaguer to this day. He went hitless in only seventeen tilts, and in 543 appearances at bat, he belted 229 safe hits for a phenomenal .422 batting average.

However, he starred with the Athletics for only one season before he was sent to the Cleveland club because the owners of the Phillies had obtained an injunction against his playing in Philadelphia. That helped restore peace between the two leagues.

He was the champion batter of the American League in three of the first four seasons he played there. He hit the ball on the line with such savage fury that rival infielders never dared to field close against him because of the risk of getting skulled by his powerful smashes. In his first fifteen years in the big leagues, he never once hit below .300.

In the thirteen years Napoleon Lajoie starred for the Cleveland team, he was so sensational that the club was named after him. It came to be known as the Cleveland Naps. For five seasons he was also their player-manager. In the 1908 season he set a record for the most chances accepted by a second baseman: 988.

Lajoie played his last game when he was past forty-one. It was his 2,475th big-league contest. His legacy to baseball was 3,251 hits, 1,503 runs, 396 stolen bases, and a lifetime batting average of .339.

So graceful a ballplayer had he been that when he was sixty years old, the American League lured him out of retirement to star in an educational motion picture demonstrating proper and graceful form at bat and in fielding.

Although an unkind fate denied the greatest of all second basemen the glory of ever playing on a pennant-winning team, he nevertheless achieved a glory unique among baseball's immortals. Only he in the Hall of Fame is now remembered for his incomparable grace. The unique inscription on his plaque reads: "Great hitter and most graceful and effective second baseman."

EDDIE COLLINS

He Won a Footrace

One of the most remarkable second basemen—and the most durable —was Edward Trowbridge ("Cocky") Collins, who performed with wizardry for 25 years. No American League player has ever been active for that length of time. And few have given the fans as many thrills.

Collins wasn't a man of large stature (5-feet-9, 170 pounds), but he was overwhelming in performance. In his quarter of a century of play he came to bat 9,949 times and hit a solid .333. And once he got on base, he was swift and elusive, making things tough for pitchers, catchers, and rival infielders. Three times he led the league in stolen bases, one year swiping 81, and he totaled 743 for his career. Only one player in history ever topped him in lawful larceny.

In World Series play (when the going gets roughest for the most able of players), Collins three times hit better than .400, the only one ever to do it. He still holds the record of 14 stolen bases in Series play.

In season play, in 1912, he set an all-time record by stealing six bases in one game—and then duplicated the feat only ten days later. That incredible feat may never be equaled.

He was born in Millerton, New York, in 1887. After his high school days

were over, he enrolled at Columbia University. In his senior year, at 19, he joined the Philadelphia Athletics and played six games under the name "Eddie Sullivan," because he didn't want his mother to know that he had become a professional ballplayer. But the news leaked out and Eddie returned to Columbia to get his degree—and then embarked on his big-league career at 20.

He showed immediately that he belonged. By the time he was 22, in 1909, he was a sensational performer for the A's, batting .346 in 153 games and leading the league in fielding his position.

Eddie Collins sparked the Athletics to four pennants in five years and then, upon being traded to the Chicago White Sox, led that team to two pennants. Before being traded by Philadelphia, he was named Most Valuable Player in the league in 1914.

The cocky fellow of Irish descent was a formidable line-drive hitter all his life, in addition to being a will-o'-the-wisp on the basepaths. He was a gentle person off the field, but a ferocious competitor while the game was on. His battles with the fiery Ty Cobb, who didn't mind showing his spikes, are legendary.

He was a fine and patient left-handed hitter who took his time about everything. He chewed gum a lot and when he went to bat he always placed the wad he was chomping on atop his cap button. But if he got two strikes behind, he would detach the gum, pop it back in his mouth, and chew furiously. That became his trademark—spectators began to look for it when he came up to hit. It helped him collect 3,311 major-league hits.

In 1915, when cocky Eddie Collins was traded to the Chicago White Sox after seven glorious years with the Philadelphia club, the Windy City home-town fans also came to love and idolize him with fanatical zeal—espe-cially after he won the most memorable footrace in World Series history.

In the 1917 post-season classic for the baseball championship against the New York Giants, in the last inning of the final game, swift and smart Eddie was perched on third base when he suddenly decided to try to steal home. Caught in a rundown play between third and home, elusive Collins jockeyed back and forth until he inveigled the Giants' famous third baseman, Heinie Zimmerman, to chase him all the way home across the plate. Speedy Eddie scored the winning run that won that World Series championship for the White Sox.

Eventually, second baseman Eddie Collins became the playing manager of the White Sox, but after twelve seasons of starring for them, he returned to the Philadelphia Athletics to play his final four years in the majors. He quit, as an active player, at the age of 43.

His love for baseball was still so impellent, however, that he remained in the majors as a coach and club executive for 15 more years.

At 52, Eddie Collins was given official recognition as an all-time second baseman wizard. The gates of the Hall of Fame swung open for him, and he was enshrined as a baseball immortal.

Ironically, the once-fabulous Eddie Collins is perhaps best remembered as one of the game's heroes only because he was the victor in a footrace that won a World Series championship for his team.

Such is fame.

FRANKIE FRISCH

The Fordham Flash

Frankie Frisch became known as the "Fordham Flash" because he went directly from the halls of Fordham University to the big leagues to play for the New York Giants, and because he played such a matchless brand of second base.

When he was inducted into the baseball Hall of Fame, his credentials as a never-to-be forgotten hero were immaculate. In his nineteen years in the major leagues as a second baseman, he had starred in 2,311 games, connected with 2,880 hits, made 4,876 putouts and 7,105 assists, batted in 1,242 runs, and wound up with a .316 lifetime batting average. He was the only second baseman in history to accept as many chances as 1,037 in a single season—a record that still stands.

Moreover, the "Fordham Flash" was such a sound baseball strategist that he was a playing manager for the last five years of his dazzlingly active major-league career, and a bench manager for eleven seasons thereafter.

Frank Frisch was born in Ozone Park, New York, in 1898. His father was a prosperous linen importer who moved his family to the Bronx, where schoolboy Frankie soon drew attention as an all-around athlete, first at Fordham Prep, and then at Fordham University. He was a brilliant shortstop in

baseball, an outstanding halfback in football, and a star speedy forward in basketball. Though he was good enough in college football to win All-America honors, his first love was always baseball.

He was always a dangerous switch-hitter at bat, had an aggressive style on the field, and was a daring base runner with a headfirst slide into bases that thrilled and delighted everyone who saw it. These qualities drew the attention of fabled New York Giants' manager John McGraw, who offered the 20-year-old youngster a contract.

Though Frisch's father wasn't altogether pleased at his son's decision to play baseball, and argued ("What kind of foolish thing is that, Frankie, chasing a ball around for a living?"), he didn't stand in his son's way. Frank Frisch joined the Giants in 1919, and was so impressive from the outset that he never had to play in the minors even for one day, or one game.

Frisch battled his way to the regular second-base post by being as aggressive as he had been at Fordham in college football. He pounced on balls hit to his field with a fervor, and even when lightning balls bounced off his chest, he had a knack of pursuit seldom seen anywhere. Frisch once explained that he didn't care about a smooth fielding technique at second base, and that his motto was: "Get the ball!"

And get them he did, for eight years, with such skill that he sparked the New York Giants to four consecutive National League pennants (1921-1924). In those four straight World Series classics, Frisch, who had become captain of the Giants' team, hit .300, .471, .400,

and .333. In the first World Series game he ever played in, the entire Giants' team made only five hits, and Frisch collected four of them.

After eight sensational seasons, McGraw and Frisch had a falling-out over a trifling incident. The fiery manager traded his equally fiery second baseman to the St. Louis Cardinals for the legendary second baseman Rogers Hornsby, a trade that created a storm of anger in St. Louis. Hornsby's shoes were difficult ones to fill for Frankie Frisch, but he quickly won over the hostile Cardinal fans with a dazzling first season by hitting .337, stealing 48 bases, and fielding with matchless and magnificent skill.

The "Fordham Flash" sparked the Cards to three pennants—in 1928, 1930, and 1931. Then, in 1934, just a year after he had become their playing manager, he piloted the rollicking "Gas House Gang," as the St. Louis Cardinals had become known, to another National League pennant, and the World Series championship, too. During this new period of glory, another of Frisch's memorable achievements was belting the first home run ever hit for the National League in the annual All-Star Game. He performed that feat in 1933.

The "Fordham Flash" retired as a player in 1937, but continued as a manager for twelve more years. He also piloted the Pittsburgh Pirates and the Chicago Cubs.

Finally, he left the majors when he was 53 years old, to busy himself with other ventures and live quietly at his Rhode Island home where he could peacefully tend his flower beds.

He died at 70, and many a fan who had seen the "Fordham Flash" in action, daringly sliding into bases head-first, conjured up a picture of Frankie Frisch sliding into Heaven that way, safe as usual.

ERNIE BANKS
The Boy Who Didn't Like Baseball

"What a great day for a ball game!"

That became the identifying cry of Ernie Banks during his nineteen years with the Chicago Cubs, and he used it to greet his teammates, manager, coaches, sportswriters and anybody else within hearing distance. It usually was a great day for him.

But what is surprising about it all is that when Ernie was a boy growing up in Dallas, Texas, he had little interest in the game. He was a versatile athlete who was captain of his high school football and basketball teams, and who ran a 52-second quarter-mile for the track team, but baseball didn't grab him at all. In fact, his father, a one-time semi-pro baseball player, had to bribe Ernie with dimes just to play catch.

In time, all of that changed as the personable Banks made his mark in the big time. He grew to love the game so much that he couldn't wait to get to the

ballpark. And when he did, his first words were:

"What a great day for a ball game!"

Despite his boyhood reservations, Banks first signed to play for a professional black team for fifteen dollars a game. He was only 17, and for five years he lived the seamy life of an obscure small-time pro ballplayer. He played in shabby parks, ate in greasy one-arm joints, and slept in flea-ridden hotels. Several times he was on the point of quitting, but each time his father talked him out of it.

Then, at 22, he was signed by the Chicago Cubs, and thus began one of the most memorable careers in big-league history. Late in the 1953 season, the manager came to Banks, clapped him on the shoulder, and said: "You're starting the game today, Ernie. Good luck!"

Banks nervously jogged out to take his position at shortstop and was never out of the lineup for the ensuing 424 games until an infected hand sidelined him. That streak set the all-time record for consecutive games played after breaking into the majors.

It wasn't long before other records were being shattered. Ernie Banks set the all-time one-season mark for highest fielding average by a shortstop—.985 —and another record for fewest errors by a shortstop—only 12 in 802 chances handled in 155 games.

Brilliant as he was in the field as a swift and ranging shortstop, he was even more wondrous with the bat. Five times he hit 40 or more home runs a season. One season he set the all-time record for shortstops by belting 44. Another season he hit 47 to lead the league. In 1955, Ernie achieved a slug-

ging feat which no one had seen in 80 years: he hit five bases-loaded grand-slam homers! His total of 293 homers represented more than that of any other shortstop in history.

Ernie Banks became one of the most popular and unusual players Chicago fans had ever idolized. When he was only in his fourth season as an established star, the home-town fans planned an "Ernie Banks Day" for him. But modest Ernie rejected the honor, saying: "I don't deserve a special day until I've fully proved myself as a true big-leaguer. I haven't been in the majors long enough for that."

It was years later that he finally accepted an "Ernie Banks Day" staged in the Chicago Cubs' ballpark. More than 50,000 home-town fans wildly acclaimed him.

Shortstop-wonder Banks was an incredible ballplayer. In 1961, when he was past thirty, the Cubs' manager asked him to switch to first base, probably because he thought Banks was slowing up at short. Ernie not only became one of the best first basemen, but he began setting new records. He set the major-league record of chances accepted by a first baseman in one game (23). Another season, he led the league's first basemen in double plays, just as he once had led the league's shortstops in twin-killings.

He was a baseball hero for many honors. In 1958, he won the National League's Most Valuable Player Award, and repeated in 1959. Being an MVP winner two years in succession was an achievement no other player had ever accomplished. Also, he was chosen for the annual All-Star Game ten times— five times as shortstop, and five times as first baseman. It was unprecedented in All-Star Game history.

Ernie Banks finally quit playing in 1971, at the age of forty. By then, he had an outstanding record, having played in 2,528 games, made 9,421 appearances at bat, collected 2,528 safe hits for 4,706 total bases, 1,305 runs, 1,636 runs-batted-in, and 512 home runs.

To be sure, Ernie Banks had come a long way from those boyhood days in Texas when he had no love for baseball, and when his father had to slip him nickels and dimes just to play catch with him.

For nineteen glorious years, Ernie Banks made his mark in big-league baseball history. And every day was for him a great day for a ball game.

HAROLD ["Pie"] TRAYNOR

Pie on the Hot Corner

Since big-league baseball began, hundreds of players have come along to play third base. But of all of them, the greatest was Harold Joseph ("Pie") Traynor.

He was as close to perfection as any third baseman had ever been. In the seventeen seasons he played for the Pittsburgh Pirates (1920-1937), he set the standard for the ultimate in third-base skill.

Born in Framingham, Massachusetts, the son of a printer, he was encouraged by his nonathletic father to take part in all sports. Young Traynor developed into a fine baseball, football, and hockey player. But as the boy grew older, baseball gradually crowded out

all the other sports. He came to be known as "Pie" because of his outstanding skill as a local baseball player. Whenever he played ball with the older and bigger boys on the playground of a parochial school, and his team won, the neighborhood priest who acted as umpire would reward the triumphant players with tasty treats. When asked what he would have, he would invariably reply, "I'll have a piece of pie, Father." The nickname stayed with him to the end of his baseball days.

Before Pie Traynor was fifteen, he appeared on a big-league diamond. But he sneaked into that thrilling moment of glory. He was watching the Boston Red Sox in a practice session one day.

When their third baseman left his position for several minutes, the youngster dashed onto the field as a "replacement." He actually worked out with the Red Sox infield for a few minutes before the startled manager of the team spotted him and chased him off the field.

A couple of years later, at seventeen, Pie Traynor was chased out of a big-league ballpark for a second time, when he tried out with the old Boston Braves. Their manager took one look at the lanky, skinny fellow and told him to go home, never come back, and forget about playing for his Braves or any other big-league team.

But two years later, Pie Traynor did come back to play in the majors. The Pittsburgh Pirates had bought him from the minor leagues for $10,000. That was in 1920.

Although he was somewhat tall for a third baseman (he stood 6 feet, 1 inch), rangy Pie Traynor nevertheless began to astonish the baseball world with electrifying performances at the hot corner of the infield. As the Pirates' third-base guardian, he conceded nothing. Flashing the quickest hands a third baseman ever had, he made incredible fielding plays on all balls hit in his direction. Gracefully, with gloved or bare hand, he speared the hardest-hit line drives at the baseline, plucked fouls out of the stands, stole ground balls from the shortstop and pop flies from the outfielder, scooped up bunts on the run, and rifled his throws to first with the most powerful throwing arm ever featured by a third baseman. And he combined his incomparable fielding skills with the best and most consistent hitting ever achieved by a third baseman.

In his seventeen years in the majors, over a span of 1,941 games and 7,558 appearances at bat, he made 2,416 safe hits, more than any other third baseman in history, and he posted a lifetime batting average of .320—the highest mark of all third basemen now in the Hall of Fame.

The first third baseman to play in as many as 1,941 major-league games, only he ever made more than 300 assists in a single season three times. He set the pace for third-base play by compiling a career total of 3,517 assists plus 2,323 putouts. His matchless playing sparked the Pirates to their very first World Series championship.

Pie Traynor's legendary career came to a sudden end when he was still a pacemaker at thirty-four. One day, during a tight ball game, he slid into home plate on a close play. But on that final play, the rival catcher landed heavily with both knees on Traynor's extended right arm. Pie's mighty throwing arm was never the same again.

He finished in the big leagues as the player-manager of the Pittsburgh Pirates. After six years, he gave up managing and quietly bowed off the baseball stage forever.

To this day, however, no man anywhere has developed into Pie Traynor's third-base equal. He has remained the unchallenged master, setting a standard for playing the hot corner that will always be used as the ultimate measure.

Perhaps for all baseball time, Pie Traynor's name will be synonymous with third base.

JOHN ["Home Run"] BAKER
Winning in the Clutch

Modern-day fans who visit baseball's Hall of Fame at Cooperstown may well wonder why, of all the players honored there, John Franklin Baker is the only one identified on his bronze plaque with the sobriquet of "Home Run" Baker.

Curiously, in his playing days, third baseman Baker never hit more than twelve home runs in any season, and in his entire fifteen years in the big leagues, he hit only 92 homers in all. Yet, only he earned the "Home Run" nickname to be linked with his real name. "Home Run" Baker acquired that unique honor by the timeliness, rather than the number, of his home runs.

It all first happened in the 1911 World Series between Connie Mack's Philadelphia Athletics and John McGraw's vaunted New York Giants, when third baseman Baker single-handedly destroyed the Giants' Hall-of-Fame pitchers Christy Mathewson and Rube Marquard with clutch home runs that won two games and paced the Athletics to the championship. The 1911 classic went down in history as the "Home Run Baker" World Series—and for the rest of his life John Baker was known only as "Home Run" Baker.

Born on a farm in Trappe, Maryland, he came to the big leagues when he was twenty-two. He was a dour left-handed batter, standing 5-feet-11, and

weighing 173 pounds. He had bowed legs and walked like a crab. Though he appeared to be awkward and graceless, he quickly revealed himself as a remarkable third baseman, a daring fielder who wasn't afraid of making an error going far out of his way to make impossible plays. He threw quickly and accurately, with tremendous speed, and despite his ungainliness, he was a superb base runner, stealing from thirty

to forty bases a season. Moreover, he was a dangerous and consistent .300-plus hitter who could belt the ball farther than any player of his time. Repeatedly, he led the American League in home runs, and his clutch homers not only helped the Philadelphia Athletics win four pennants, but won him baseball immortality.

When Connie Mack had his legendary "$100,000 infield," "Home Run" Baker was its most luminous star, acclaimed as one of the outstanding third basemen of the game.

In all, "Home Run" Baker was a fabulous hero for fifteen years, until he quit at 38 to return to his Maryland farm and be a dirt farmer again.

He left behind him an impressive record. He had played in 1,575 major-league games, connected with 1,838 hits, compiled a lifetime batting average of .307, and helped his team win six pennants—four with the Philadelphia Athletics, and two (in his final two years) with the New York Yankees.

It was enough to win for him election to the Hall of Fame as one of the never-to-be-forgotten stars of baseball.

And, until his death in 1963 at the age of 77, he was still known and honored as "Home Run" Baker. It is likely that only he will remain identified in the Hall of Fame by the "Home Run" nickname, a forceful reminder of what a unique wonder he once was.

EDDIE MATHEWS

The "Homer" of the Braves

Edwin Lee Mathews, born in Texarkana, Texas, and brought up in Santa Barbara, California, who became a superstar by smashing 512 home runs (thus also becoming one of the top homer-hitters in history), came to the major leagues by way of a high school dance, dressed in a tuxedo.

When 17-year-old Eddie Mathews was about to graduate from high school, in 1948, he was such an outstanding baseball player that no less than fourteen scouts were anxious to sign him to a contract to play in the major leagues. A rule in effect at the time provided that no scout could sign up any high school boy to a baseball contract until his senior class had graduated, so the scouts in pursuit of Eddie Mathews simply bided their time for the day of his graduation.

When that day finally came, thirteen of the big-league scouts were camped on the front porch of the Mathews' home, waiting for Eddie to come home from his senior prom. But one scout was more ingenious than the others. He was ex-major-league outfielder Jo-Jo Moore, scouting for the Boston Braves. He hied himself to the Carillo Hotel, where Eddie, dressed in a tuxedo, was dancing and celebrating. There Jo-Jo

cornered Eddie in a men's room, and there he persuaded him to sign his first contract to play professional baseball.

After seasoning in the minors for three years, Mathews came to the major leagues to play third base for the Boston Braves. He starred for them for thirteen years, as the Braves moved from Boston to Milwaukee and later to Atlanta.

He quickly served notice that he was destined for fame. In his freshman year, he belted 25 home runs, a surprising feat for a 20-year-old rookie. The following season, he really blossomed out as one of the game's mightiest sluggers, leading the National League with 47 home runs. He drove in a resounding 135 runs, while hitting over .300. Largely due to his brilliant fielding at third base and his thunderous home-run hitting, he eventually helped the Braves win two pennants and a World Series championship. Nine times he was named to the National League All-Star team in recognition of his prominence as a third baseman.

Wherever Eddie Mathews played during his 18-year career in the majors, he brought with him inspirational magic. In 1968, when he moved to another league by being traded to the Detroit Tigers, he not only continued to perform brilliantly at third base, but with his magnificent fielding and home-run slugging he helped his new team win the American League pennant, and then the World Series championship.

It was Eddie Mathews' last hurrah as a big-league standout. At the end of that season, 38-year-old Mathews hung up his uniform as a player, leaving a glorious record. He was the first third baseman to have played in as many as 2,319 major-league games, accept 6,371 fielding chances at the hot corner of the infield, make 2,966 putouts, 4,385 assists, and become the only third-sacker ever to hit 512 home runs.

As a fitting climax to his remarkable playing career, Eddie Mathews returned to the major leagues in 1972, at the age of 41. He became manager of the Atlanta Braves, the same team with which he had started his journey to greatness.

HONUS WAGNER
The Flying Dutchman

John Peter ("Honus") Wagner, the man they called "The Flying Dutchman," was an incomparable shortstop, a wondrous hitter, a sensational base-stealer, and, according to many historians, the greatest all-round

big-league baseball player of them all. But without a doubt the greatest shortstop who ever lived.

The strange thing was that Wagner didn't even look like a major-league ballplayer. He was so bowlegged that a barrel could be rolled between his legs. His enormously long arms and huge hands hung like bunches of bananas on his 71-inch, 200-pound body, and with his bearlike frame, Honus gave the appearance of being extremely awkward. At the sight of him on a ball field, it was impossible to believe that he was destined for immortality. But once the game started, he was that and more.

As a hitter, he batted .300-plus for 17 consecutive years, setting all-time National League records for most singles (2,426) and most triples (252). He won the league batting championship eight times, a record that still stands. He made 3,430 hits, and wound up with a lifetime batting average of .329 for the 2,785 major-league games he played in.

As a fielder, "The Flying Dutchman" was unbelievable. He made seemingly impossible plays with the greatest of ease on dry fields, slipping or falling on wet fields, and far back of third. From any position, he threw like a shot from a rifle. Often he threw out runners at first while kneeling, sitting, or lying on the ground. All told, he made 7,367 putouts and 6,628 assists. His instinct was uncanny in estimating where the batter might send a certain pitch. The ball seemed to follow his glove. In completing double plays, he never had an equal. When he scooped up the ball with those huge hamlike hands and fired it to first base for a putout, the swift flight of the ball was often a dust cloud. The first baseman often said that he simply picked out the biggest object in the cloud and caught it.

For a player of his size and build, Wagner had deceptive speed. He made base running appear as simple as he did his magnificent shortstopping and mighty batting. He stole 720 bases—for six seasons he was the National League's theft leader.

Born in Carnegie, Pennsylvania, of immigrant German parents, Honus Wagner was working in the coal mines at the age of 12, loading cars in the pits. At 18, he was cutting hair as a barber, and by 21, he had become a professional baseball player in the minor leagues. He was 23 when he became a big-league shortstop for $350 a month. The most he ever got as a fabulous major-league baseball hero was $10,000 a year. Twice, his all-around playing sparked an average colorless Pittsburgh

Pirates team to pennants, and a World Series championship, too.

Throughout his 21 years in the major leagues, "The Flying Dutchman" was a modest, quiet, well-mannered player who shied away from the rough stuff that was part of the game in the early years of this century. Though a powerful man, he refused to resort to ruthless bone-breaking play. He never spiked nor knocked down a rival player deliberately, a gentle giant who played with grace and good humor, admired and loved by legions of fans.

He was a hero without pretensions. Once, he was offered a thousand dollars a week to appear on the vaudeville stage. But Honus Wagner rejected it as he simply said: "I'm no actor, and I'm no freak. I'm just another ballplayer."

His devotion to the game was overwhelming, and he played with a singleness of purpose that outshone everything else in his life. He was 43, in 1917, when he finally left the major leagues as a player.

He was 62, in 1936, when the National Baseball Hall of Fame first opened its doors as a Cooperstown shrine to welcome the immortals of the game. Only five baseball greats entered there the first year. It came as no surprise that one of the original five pillars was "The Flying Dutchman," John Peter Wagner—the greatest big-league shortstop who ever lived.

WALTER ["Rabbit"] MARANVILLE
The Merry Little Rabbit

One of the most durable players in big-league history was a colorful gay blade of a man who stood only 65 inches tall and hardly weighed 150 pounds. Famed as the "Little Rabbit," he carved a niche for himself in baseball's Hall of Fame because he was an amazing shortstop in 2,670 major-league games, over a period of twenty-three years.

Born in Springfield, Massachusetts, young Walter James Vincent Maranville played school and sandlot ball until he was 19 years old, when he became a minor-league player. Only one year later, he crashed the big leagues as a shortstop for the National League's Boston Braves. That was in 1912. He continued playing in the major leagues until he was 44 years old.

From the very start of his long career, Maranville—nicknamed "Rabbit," because of the way he hopped around an infield to snare ground balls —was a most unusual shortstop. He caught infield flies as no other shortstop ever did, with both hands held high against his body, which seemed like a comedy stunt, and called it his vest-pocket catch. He was a glove magician —smart, fast, sure-handed, aggressive, and fearless.

The Rabbit became a talented and dynamic performer who managed to supply the spark that led teams to pennants, even when it appeared those teams didn't have a prayer of winning.

His most spectacular effort came when he helped the 1914 Boston Braves —a mediocre team wallowing in last place late in the season—suddenly catch fire and win the league pennant by ten and a half games, then demolish

the mighty world-champion Philadelphia Athletics in four consecutive World Series victories. The shining hero of that never-to-be-forgotten "Miracle Team" was Rabbit Maranville. Fourteen years later, he was again the hero of another miracle pennant triumph when he led the St. Louis Cardinals to a World Series.

The impish Rabbit was a tremendous clutch player who performed best when the going was roughest. Time and again, he led all National League short-stops in fielding, chances accepted, and putouts; and though he wasn't a power hitter, he collected 2,605 safe hits for his fame.

But the Rabbit was more than one of the greatest shortstops. He was a blithe spirit who became one of the funniest and best-liked players of the baseball game. He loved to make mischief, and he always clowned to make the fans laugh. At times, he crawled through an umpire's legs to get to a base. Once, he came to bat wearing a raincoat and carrying an umbrella—to convince an umpire that it was raining hard enough to call the game. And once, on a crowded street, when he saw a famous umpire who in a game had rendered an unfavorable decision against him, the clowning Rabbit ran after him, shouting, "Stop, thief! Stop, thief!" His antic so embarrassed and confused the umpire that he took off on a run to get away from the zany Rabbit. A crowd ran after him, with Maranville at its head, believing that a real thief was trying to escape.

On a ball field, the fun-loving Rabbit performed astonishing antics for laughs. Spunky and fearless, he often defied opposing base runners by sticking his nose right into their flying spikes. He would tag out a runner coming into second, and then end up sitting triumphantly on his chest.

Off the field, the Rabbit was just as brazen in his search for laughs. A pet parrot or monkey might be perched on his shoulder when he appeared at restaurants. He kept pigeons in hotel closets, put fish in bathtubs, and allowed rabbits to scamper about in his hotel room. Once he waded into a hotel-lobby fountain, caught a goldfish, and took a bite out of it. Another time, for a lark, he bewildered and frightened his teammates by clinging to a narrow ledge outside his hotel room window—twelve floors above the ground. He was constantly doing something to enhance his reputation as a clown. Because of his tomfoolery, he drifted to five different major-league teams to continue his playing as a shortstop. At one time or other, he also became a playing manager, but clowned himself out of the pilot job.

The amazing Rabbit was 43 when he suffered a broken leg in a spring exhibition game, which idled him for the entire 1934 season. But he returned the following year to play shortstop for one more season before retiring.

It ended an incredible saga of a baseball great who, despite all of his horseplay for almost a quarter of a century, is honored as a shortstop immortal.

JOE CRONIN

A Long Way on the Glory Road

In 1974, Joe Cronin climaxed his remarkable and unique 48-year career in big-league baseball by becoming Chairman of the Board of Directors of the American League, the highest and most prestigious executive post ever achieved by a one-time major-league player. Along the way, he had been one of the game's greatest shortstops, a pennant-winning manager, the president of a major league, and one of the immortal tenants in the Hall of Fame at Cooperstown. It is a rags-to-riches baseball classic that is stranger than fiction.

Born in San Francisco in 1906, the son of a teamster, Joseph Edward Cronin played sandlot, high school, and semi-pro baseball before crashing the big leagues at 19 as a shortstop for the Pittsburgh Pirates. Though he was a strong hitter, he was so ungainly and awkward a shortstop that, after playing

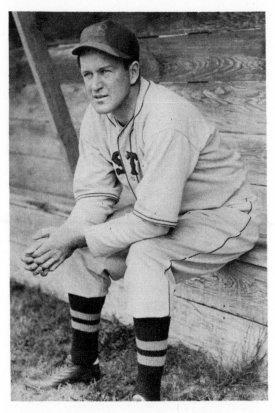

in only fifty games, he was cast adrift and shipped to the minor leagues.

At Kansas City, in the American Association, Joe Cronin was spotted by a Washington Senators' scout who was so impressed by his hitting that he bought him (for a cheap price) for the club. But the Senators' owner, Clark ("The Fox") Griffith, was furious when he saw what his scout had delivered. The scout tried to "butter up" the angry club owner by telling him: "I not only brought you a promising shortstop, but also a fine Irish lad as a husband for your daughter."

Sure enough, within his first few seasons with the Washington Senators, the gangling, awkward, and square-jawed Irishman from California, by dint of tenacious practice and fierce dedication, not only developed into one of the most expert fielding shortstops in the game's history, but he and the club

owner's daughter, Mildred, fell in love and were married, to live happily ever after, just as it happens in storybooks.

Dramatically, Joe Cronin became the American League's Most Valuable Player, hitting over .300 and making more putouts and more assists than any other shortstop. Seven times he led his league in chances accepted, an indication that he was a fielder who covered an unusually large area. His record for lifetime putouts and assists has never been topped.

Then, in the fall of 1932, a few days before his twenty-sixth birthday, Cronin was named manager of the Washington Senators. And in 1933, his very first season as a playing manager, he piloted the Senators to a pennant. He was promptly dubbed "the boy-wonder manager." He was the youngest flag-winning manager in big-league history.

But to everyone's astonishment, after the following season, his father-in-law, Clark Griffith, sold him to the Boston Red Sox for $250,000—the highest price ever paid for one major-league player. Shortstop Joe Cronin played with and managed the Red Sox for the following eleven years, and piloted them to a pennant, too. His dazzling career as a shortstop came to a sudden end in 1945, when he broke a leg.

Throughout his playing days, Cronin was a tremendous and dangerous hitter. In 2,074 games, appearing at bat 7,577 times, he made 2,285 hits, winding up with a lifetime batting average of .300-plus. At times, he produced astonishing feats with his bat. The most unforgettable one for the record book happened during the 1943 season. In each game of an important double-header his team was playing, with two mates aboard and the game in the balance, manager Cronin sent himself up to bat as a pinch-hitter. And each time he belted a winning home run. That season he established an all-time homer record for pinch-hitting that still stands, slugging five pinch-hitting home runs. As a major-league player, shortstop Joe Cronin was good enough to win membership in the National Hall of Fame.

In 1948, after he wound up his illustrious career as a player and manager, Joe Cronin moved into the front office of the Boston Red Sox club as its vice-president and general manager. He stayed there until 1959, when, to no one's surprise, Cronin was elected president of the American League. It was an unprecedented achievement—he was the first and only ex-major-league player ever to attain that high a baseball post. He held it with honor until 1974, when he moved to an even more exalted position—chairman of the board of directors of the American League.

It was the climax of a remarkable and glorious 48-year career in baseball for the once-gangling, awkward, and ungainly 19-year-old shortstop, unwanted by his first major-league team, and rejected as a misfit player.

LUCIUS ["Luke"] APPLING

"Ol' Aches and Pains"

The two things that marked Luke Appling's brilliant 20-year career with the Chicago White Sox were (1) his ability to foul off pitches whenever he felt like it and (2) his knack of getting hurt, or imagining that he was hurt, to the point that he was known around the league as "Ol' Aches and Pains" Appling. The ailments never seemed to bother Luke, once the game got under way.

For years Appling was the best hit-and-run man in the majors. He was a master at hitting behind the runner at first, and if he didn't get the precise outside pitch he wanted, he was able to foul off as many as a dozen deliveries until he did. Fans often chanted the count in unison as he deliberately spoiled pitches ("One," "Two," "Three," etc.), and it wasn't unusual for them to reach numbers like 10 and 12. He was particularly adept with two strikes on him, and there were occa-

fashion, and hobbling around fast enough to get the extra base.

One day he slid into second awkwardly, beating the throw to the base. But when the dust cleared, Ol' Aches and Pains was writhing on the ground, moaning that his leg was broken. Everybody chuckled, including the second-base umpire.

"Come on, quit faking, Luke!" the Sox manager growled. "Hey, you're cluttering up the field!" grinned the rival second baseman. "Come on, play ball!" ordered the umpire. But this time Luke really had a broken leg and it put him out of action for half a season.

Appling was born in High Point, North Carolina, but grew up in Atlanta, Georgia, where he played sandlot ball and attended nearby Oglethorpe University. A scout found him there and, at 21, he went from the campus to the Atlanta Crackers of the Southern Association. But before he had completed his first season in the minors, he was brought up to the big leagues to play shortstop for the Chicago White Sox. He remained with them for twenty consecutive years.

Once he was in the majors, it didn't take long for Luke Appling to establish himself. For an unprecedented seven times he led all league shortstops in putouts, and he set another major-league mark for assists.

Hypochondriac that he was all through his career, and despite the real or imaginary pains and ailments, Luke Appling accomplished feats never achieved by any other shortstop-great in history. Only he ever played at shortstop in as many as 2,422 major-league games, and only he accepted as many as 11,569 chances. His lifetime putouts

sions when he stayed at bat for five minutes or longer until the pitcher was worn out and either walked him or gave him his pitch.

He was also a superlative shortstop for his long tenure with the White Sox, despite his run of complaints that his ankles or his back or his neck were hurting. Somehow, once the game started, Luke was always making the brilliant play or getting the key hit that beat the other side. In 1936, for instance, when he was having more physical trouble than usual (according to him), he won the batting championship with a mark of .388. It was the highest mark ever achieved by a third baseman. Seven years later, still wracked with pain, he won the title again.

Most of the time, Luke's managers took his complaints with tongue in cheek. No matter how loudly he complained, Appling was always there in the starting lineup, getting his singles and doubles, fielding in spectacular reached 4,349, and assists 7,220. He wound up with a .310 lifetime batting mark for his twenty years of effort.

"Ol' Aches and Pains" finally quit in 1950, at the age of 41. Fourteen years later, in testimony of his true greatness as a shortstop, he was elected to the National Baseball Hall of Fame, ever to be honored and remembered.

Even on that special day, Luke Appling remained true to his nickname of "Ol' Aches and Pains." Baseball's prime hypochondriac told a huge crowd acclaiming him:

"My election to the Hall of Fame overshadows all my other thrills in baseball. I've had other great honors, but nothing like this. . . . But, gee," Luke Appling added with a wink, placing his hand on his back, "I wish I wasn't aching and hurting so much on this great day."

BROOKS ROBINSON
Mr. Impossible

In 1974, when Brooks Robinson was thirty-seven years old and had embarked on his twentieth season with the Baltimore Orioles, he could already look back on an incredible record of statistics he had compiled as the most durable major-league third baseman of all time.

He had played third base in more major-league games than anyone: 2,504. Nine times he had led the American League in games played at third base— a record. Ten times he had led the league in fielding average at third—another all-time record. He had made most double plays at third, for a lifetime record of 535. He had made the most assists at third, lifetime, 971; and the most putouts, lifetime, 2,436. Thirteen times in a row he had won the coveted "Golden Glove" award given annually to the best fielding third baseman in the game. And seventeen times in a row he had been chosen to play third base in the annual All-Star Game. Also, he had gained for his fame the Most Valuable Player award.

Astonishing statistics, however, don't tell the whole story of Brooks Calbert Robinson's true greatness as a baseball hero.

Born in Little Rock, Arkansas, he went through high school and a brief stay at the Little Rock Junior College

before his ambition turned him to professional baseball.

He was not yet 18 when the Baltimore Orioles signed him to his first big-league contract. But after playing only six games and making only two safe hits, young Robinson was shipped off to the minors for more seasoning. A year later, the Orioles brought him back. Again after playing in only 15 games and making only ten safe hits, Robinson was returned to the minors for more seasoning. When he was twenty years old, however, the tenacious and determined Brooks Robinson returned to the major leagues to stay, embarking on a saga unknown to any other third baseman.

The six-feet-one 190-pounder from Little Rock, who threw and batted right-handed, began to field at the hot corner of the infield like a ring-tailed wonder. He refused to give up fielding any ball hit anywhere near him, often going deep into the shortstop hole to snare vicious drives with breathtaking ease. He began making spectacular plays at third that had to be seen to be believed. It earned for him the nickname of "Mr. Impossible." He became one of the smoothest third basemen the game had ever known—a marvel who made the most dramatic plays routine. As the seasons went by, Brooks Robinson became not only the premier all-around third baseman of his time, but also perhaps the greatest of any time in baseball history. He inspired the Baltimore Orioles to pennants and World Series championships. And in every World Series battle, third baseman Robinson gave memorable performances.

In 1974, at the age of 37, "Mr. Impossible" was still starring in the major leagues, continuing to perform his fielding miracles at the hottest corner of the infield, and enriching his fame.

TINKER-to-EVERS-to-CHANCE
The Deadliest Twin-Killers

At the start of the 1902 major-league season, the famous first baseman and playing manager of the Chicago Cubs astonished the baseball world by installing two 21-year-old rookies in the Cubs' infield. One was shortstop Joe Tinker, 69 inches tall and 175 pounds heavy. The other was Johnny Evers, 69 inches tall and barely 135 pounds heavy.

Those two Cub rookies, with first baseman Frank Chance, became the most colorful, most glamorous, most efficient, and greatest double-play combination in big-league history. The trio became so identified for their twin-killings that everyone came to believe that they actually had invented the double play. Poets and songwriters went lyrical about them, to foster the legend of Tinker-to-Evers-to-Chance. The most popular ditty of the time went like this:

These are the saddest of possible
    words,
  Tinker-to-Evers-to-Chance,
Trio of Bear Cubs fleeter than birds,
  Tinker-to-Evers-to-Chance,
Ruthlessly pricking our gonfalon
    bubble,
  Making a Giant hit into a double,
Words that are weighty with nothing
    but trouble,
  Tinker-to-Evers-to-Chance.

The trio did more than any other three players to dramatize major-league play as America's favorite pastime, and put big-league baseball into the more important money as a national sport.

Joe Tinker came from Muscatah, Kansas, and he was the most light-hearted of that famed trio. He was a standout shortstop during his twelve years with the Chicago Cubs, and five times he led the National League shortstops in fielding. One of the most fearless of big-league players, he was also a dangerous clutch hitter.

Johnny Evers came from Troy, New York. Despite his puny size, he was a bundle of dynamite. Nicknamed "The Crab," he was a pugnacious and flawless player at the keystone bag, with the quickest brain in the game. He feared no one, and was ever ready to tangle and trade fists with the biggest bullies in the majors. During his twelve seasons with the Cubs, he was a whiz on the bases. He stole 325 for his fame.

Frank Chance was a college product from Fresno, California. Though he became the greatest first baseman of his time, he gained even greater fame as the player-manager of the Chicago Cubs. "Peerless Leader" they called him. With Joe Tinker and Johnny Evers

Frank Chance

Johnny Evers

Joe Tinker

in the infield, he piloted the Cubs to four pennants and two World Series championships in five years (1906-1910).

A big, raw-boned, bowlegged, 200-pound six-footer, Frank Chance was a dangerous hitter during his eighteen years in the majors. He was so feared by enemy pitchers that he was "beaned" more often than any other major-league player of his time. One Memorial Day, during a double-header, he was "beaned" for a record five times. Frank Chance was struck by pitched balls so often during his career that it contributed to his loss of hearing and his early death at 47 years of age.

Tinker-to-Evers-to-Chance was a strange double-play combination for their legendary fame. When off the

field, Frank Chance completely ignored his famous shortstop and second baseman. As for infielders Joe Tinker and Johnny Evers, although they played flawlessly side by side for twelve years, they never spoke a word to each other, because of a feud, when they were off the playing field.

And, like Frank Chance, both Johnny Evers and Joe Tinker were destined for tragedy when their playing days were over. Joe Tinker lost a leg, and Johnny Evers became a wheelchair invalid for the rest of his life.

The fabulous trio remained bound together in glory, however. In 1946, all three had their last "hurrah" as Tinker-to-Evers-to-Chance. All three, as if they were one, were enshrined in baseball's Hall of Fame.

MEN BEHIND MASKS

ROGER BRESNAHAN
The First Immortal Backstop

Roger Philip Bresnahan was the first catcher to gain the supreme baseball honor of placement in the Cooperstown Hall of Fame.

Born in Toledo, Ohio, he came off the sandlots to pitch for the old Washington team in the National League before he had even celebrated his eighteenth birthday. It was 1897.

He was 68 inches tall, tough, extremely aggressive, unusually strong, swift of foot, a tricky base runner, and a powerful hitter. After pitching only seven games for the Washington club, and winning four, he left the team be-cause the club would not pay him the salary he wanted. He went back to Toledo. By the time he returned to the big leagues three years later to play for the legendary Baltimore Orioles, he was both a pitcher and a catcher.

But after he spent two seasons with the Orioles, his teammate, third-base-man John McGraw, jumped to the National League to become manager of the New York Giants, and Bresnahan went along. In New York, Bresnahan served not only as a pitcher and a catcher, but as a third baseman, short-stop, outfielder, and assistant manager,

too. Finally, he settled down primarily as a catcher.

He had wondrous years starring for the Giants. He was an unusually brainy backstop—a schemer and a scrapper beyond compare. He hit hard, as high as .350, and stole as many as 35 bases a season. Because of his remarkable speed, he often batted first in the lineup, a role rarely ever given to any other big-league catcher. Moreover, "Duke," as they nicknamed him, caught for all the great Giant pitchers of his time—and to perfection.

That blue-eyed, brown-haired, handsome little man of Irish descent was absolutely fearless. He was skillful at working a rival pitcher for a walk, and never feared getting nicked by a pitch in order to get such a free walk.

Once, in a 1907 game, Duke was beaned by a pitch from the famous Cincinnati Reds' hurler, Andy Coakley. The ball caught Bresnahan behind the ear, and he fell unconscious. The injury seemed so severe that he was given last rites at home plate. But, 30 days later, he recovered and returned to the Giants' line-up.

By a strange coincidence, the first pitcher he faced at bat was Andy Coakley, who had nearly killed him. Although two brush-back pitches were fired at him during that game, the fearless catcher hit two doubles for his afternoon's work.

An innovation brought to big-league baseball by the ingenious Roger Bresnahan was shinguards for a catcher. He appeared behind home plate one afternoon wearing a pair of white shinguards outside his stockings. Though the players and amused baseball fans derided him with taunts, Bresnahan continued to wear the shinguards whenever he toiled behind home plate. Eventually, no big-league catcher, if he had sense, appeared for play without wearing shinguards.

After seven seasons as a catcher for the Giants and helping them win two pennants, Duke left the team to become the playing manager of the St. Louis Cardinals. Then, after four seasons, he drifted to the Chicago Cubs to serve one season as their player-manager before quitting the major leagues at the age of 36.

He left behind an impressive record for his fame as the first outstanding big-league catcher in history. He had back-stopped in 1,410 games and collected 1,251 hits.

He returned to Toledo and became a baseball club owner by buying the local "Mud Hens," then playing in the American Association.

In 1945, a year after his death, a unique honor was bestowed upon the fabulous little catcher. Roger Bresnahan arrived at the Hall of Fame at Cooperstown, the first major-league catcher to be so elected.

BILL DICKEY
Just Plain Bill

The major-league backstop who came closest to being the perfect catcher was Bill Dickey. All during his seventeen years of toiling as a backstop for the once-fabulous New York Yankees—he caught in 1,827 games—unobtrusive, colorless, hardworking catcher Bill Dickey had to play in the shadow of some of the most glamorous stars in baseball history. He was known as Just Plain Bill. Yet he accomplished enough to be acclaimed as the perfect catcher, and to enter baseball's immortal Hall of Fame.

Born in Bastrop, Louisiana, William Malcolm Dickey received his first baseball lessons from his father, a railroad conductor who once had been a minor-league catcher. Before he was 18, Bill Dickey had become so outstanding a catcher for semi-pro baseball teams around Hot Springs, Arkansas, where the family had settled, that he caught the eye of the manager of the Little

Rock club in the Southern Association. Dickey became a minor-league catcher, playing in the minors for four years, until the New York Yankees bought him for $12,500 in 1928.

When the Yankee manager first saw

the rookie catcher behind the plate, happily, he told the unimpressed Yankee club owner: "We've bought a player who'll become the greatest catcher in the game." Bill Dickey became just that.

There never was a catcher in the major leagues more durable than Bill Dickey. For 13 consecutive seasons, he caught more than 100 games a season. He never complained, and rarely missed a game because of his physical injuries. Once, after a severe beaning sent him to a hospital, hard-working Bill Dickey was back in the Yankee lineup only a few days later.

His finesse as a catcher was incomparable. He seldom called a wrong pitch, and once he spotted a rival batter's weakness, he never forgot. The many Yankee pitchers who gained fame during his time gave Dickey much of the credit for their victories.

A superb defensive catcher with a rifle arm, he led his league in assists time and again. The foremost base-stealers came to fear him so much that they refrained from their larceny whenever Dickey was the Yankees' backstop.

At the plate with a bat in hand, he was feared, too. Season after season, he batted more than .300, hit 202 home runs, and collected a total of 1,969 hits for a lifetime batting average of .313. His magnificent catching and powerful hitting were instrumental in helping the Yankees win eight pennants and seven World Series championships. Yet, through all that glory, Bill Dickey remained so modest and unobtrusive that his greatness was taken for granted.

Only once in his 17 major-league years did this quiet and most gentlemanly of big-league players crash the headlines. It was when he triggered one of the wildest free-for-all brawls to take place on a baseball diamond.

One July afternoon in the 1932 season a tough Washington Senators' player named Carl Reynolds came barreling into home plate, deliberately crashing into catcher Dickey and sending him sprawling. For the first and only time, "Just Plain Bill" lost his temper, got up, and threw a punch at Reynolds. It broke his jaw, and a memorable donnybrook ensued between the players of both teams. Even a number of fans joined the brawl, which lasted for almost an hour before it was quelled.

For his involvement, Bill Dickey was fined a thousand dollars and suspended for thirty days. It was the most severe penalty to be imposed on a major-league player for fighting. Dickey always regretted that outburst, and never again raised a hand in anger, no matter what the provocation.

Before the 1943 season was fully over, though he batted .351 and he was 36 years old, he enlisted in the United States Navy, because World War II was on. He was gone from the major leagues for two years. When he returned, he played one more season for the Yankees, then quit as a big-league catcher.

Looking back at his career, Hall-of-Famer Bill Dickey once said: "A catcher must want to catch if he hopes to achieve big-league greatness." And that's what Bill Dickey did for seventeen brilliant years, to win acclaim from a legion of baseball admirers and historians as "the perfect catcher."

LAWRENCE ["Yogi"] BERRA
The Miracle of the Ugly Duckling

In 1946, when 21-year-old Lawrence Peter Berra came out of service with the United States Navy to become a catcher for the New York Yankees, he looked neither like a sailor nor a baseball player. He was a funny-looking, chunky, knock-kneed, thick-shouldered, 68-inch guy who waddled like a duck when walking. He was homely and almost illiterate. He looked like a comic-strip character. If ever a major-league rookie was an ugly duckling, he was Yogi Berra, born in St. Louis, Missouri, the son of an Italian immigrant bricklayer.

From early boyhood he had been a sandlot baseball player. His buddies had tagged him "Yogi," an appellation intended to describe an oddball. He never lost that nickname for his identity in the baseball world.

At 17, Yogi so impressed a Yankees' baseball scout that he was given a pro contract to play in the low minors at ninety dollars a month until such time as the fabled New York club needed him. Yogi played for a couple of years in the minors, until he joined the Navy for World War II military service.

At the beginning of his big-league career, the squat, homely Yogi Berra was a ludicrous specimen as a catcher.

Awkward to a fault, he misjudged fly balls, dropped easy pops, fell down chasing bunts, and threw wildly to bases. His stance at bat was most peculiar, and he swung at all bad pitches.

Once, when his annoyed manager bawled him out for not thinking by swinging at bad pitches, Yogi defended himself by saying: "Gee, skipper, how can I think and hit at the same time?"

When the famous Yankee coach, immortal Hall-of-Fame catcher Bill Dickey, began to tutor Yogi in the art of big-league catching, the unschooled rookie, who had never even completed grade school, happily informed everyone: "Coach Dickey is learning me all his experience."

Because of his homely looks, his childlike gullibility, and his innocently funny verbal boners, Yogi became a target for ridicule and cruel taunts from rival players. But good-natured, easygoing Yogi merely shrugged off the abuse with a friendly smile and plugged on tirelessly, learning all there was to know about being a backstop. He learned quickly and well.

As the baseball seasons passed, Yogi Berra rose from ugly-duckling status to full-fledged stardom. He flowered into one of the smartest, most durable, and best fielding catchers in the majors. He also became a most dangerous clutch hitter.

Only he ever played in 148 consecutive games without committing an error. He set the all-time mark for most chances accepted by a catcher (9,043), and most putouts by a catcher (9,194). He became the first big-league backstop to play in more than 2,000 games, and the first to collect 2,000 hits. His lifetime total reached 2,150 safe hits. He hit more home runs than any other catcher in history—358.

Four years in a row he topped the mark of 100 runs-batted-in, and his lifetime total was 1,430. For fifteen successive years, catcher Yogi was picked by the American League to play in the annual All-Star Game against the best players in the National League. He became the first catcher to win the annual Most Valuable Player Award three times.

Moreover, Yogi Berra became a baseball idol respected and admired by all, because everybody discovered that the ugly-duckling catcher was a wonderful human being with a charm and sense of humor all his own. His many funny verbal boners became treasured nuggets in baseball lore.

Yogi's magnificence as a catcher helped the New York Yankees win 14 pennants and nine World Series championships. As if that wasn't enough glory for one backstop-great, Yogi also became the greatest World Series hero in history. Only he ever played in as many as 75 classic games, connecting with more hits than any other player, 71. And no catcher ever chalked up as many putouts, assists, nor hit as many home runs in that championship battle as did Yogi Berra. He set a flock of other all-time records as kingpin of all World Series heroes.

Yogi was 40 when he quit as a catcher, but he was not yet done for baseball history. When the New York club elevated him to manage the Yankees, he promptly led them to a pennant.

Then he switched to the National League to toil as a coach for the New York Mets. In 1972 he became their manager, and the following season he piloted the Mets to a pennant. Thus, Yogi went down in history as the second manager to win a pennant in each of the two major leagues.

But perhaps the greatest joy of Yogi Berra's career came when his skill as an incomparable major-league catcher was officially recognized and honored for all time by election to baseball's Hall of Fame.

So ended the miracle of an ugly duckling who was transformed into a beautiful swan for the romance of baseball history.

ROY CAMPANELLA
The Joyous Warrior

There are four significant stages in the life of Roy Campanella as a legendary baseball hero.

At seventeen he had already left his home town of Philadelphia, Pennsylvania, to become a professional catcher in the old National Negro League, and for ten years he barnstormed all over the United States and South America, playing summer and winter, catching more than three hundred games a year for a salary of less than $300 a month.

At twenty-seven he finally arrived in the big leagues, joining the Brooklyn Dodgers. It was a historic occasion: he was the first black catcher in major-league history.

At thirty-seven his baseball career ended suddenly and shockingly when an automobile mishap left him partially paralyzed, forcing him to spend the rest of his life in a wheelchair.

And at forty-seven, he had his "last hurrah" when he entered baseball's

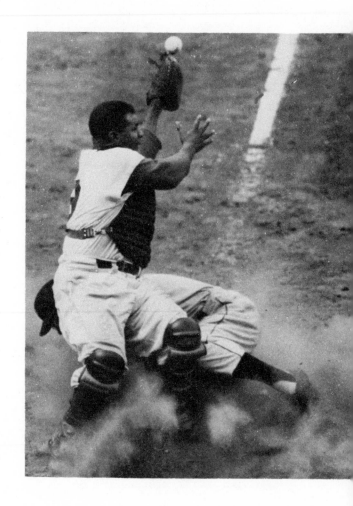

Hall of Fame as an immortal of the game.

It all began for Roy Campanella in the slum streets of Philadelphia where his dream was born—to become a famous baseball player. No youngster ever played baseball with more gusto and greater joy. He was only fifteen when a team of grown men offered him twenty-five dollars a week to be its catcher for weekend games. Roy's mother, a deeply religious woman, wouldn't let him play Sunday games at first, but a compromise was arranged. Roy could play on Sundays only if he attended church first. The owner of a barnstorming black baseball team then saw him catch, and young Roy became a full-fledged professional baseball player, traveling everywhere for most of the year. Wherever he played, he always had on hand the Bible his mother had insisted he take with him to guide him in his wanderings.

Finally, the discriminatory racial barrier existing in major-league baseball tumbled, and Roy Campanella, age 27, came to the big leagues as a catcher for the Brooklyn Dodgers.

And what a catcher he was! He was a superb handler of pitchers, a great fielder, and a fine and powerful hitter. Roly-poly Campanella was like a cat behind the plate, with an astonishing quickness to catch foul pop-ups and field bunts. He had a rifle arm, and in his first 600 major-league games he nailed 150 would-be base-stealers. He was such a brainy catcher that no pitcher, however great, ever shook him off on a signal of what to pitch to a batter.

A natural leader, he survived an assortment of injuries to achieve stardom as one of the greatest baseball heroes of his time.

He was the most joyous player the majors ever had, for he caught every game with the ecstasy of a man who loved his work. Affable, easygoing, and with merry laughter pouring out of him for friend or foe, Roy Campanella became one of the most popular players on the diamond.

His hitting was never in doubt. He stroked 30 or more homers a season, four times. He was the first catcher to wallop 41 home runs in a single season, and the only catcher ever with 142 runs-batted-in for a single season. In the ten years he starred in the majors, he belted 242 home runs.

He was the first catcher in National League history to play in one hundred or more games for nine consecutive seasons. One season, he set an astonishing all-time record with 807 putouts, and led the league in putouts six times. He made the All-Star team every year of his major-league career—and so versatile was he as a phenomenal backstop that he won the Most Valuable Player Award three times. In his ten years with the Brooklyn Dodgers, he sparked them to five pennants.

After playing in 1,215 major-league games and collecting 1,161 hits, the seemingly indestructible Roy Campanella suddenly came to the end of the glory road. He was 37, and still at the height of his fame as one of baseball's greatest catchers, when an automobile crackup on a lonely road late at night left him with a broken neck and partial paralysis. He would live the rest of his life in a wheelchair, and never play baseball again.

Campy's courageous fight to survive

as a useful individual stirred the heart of the entire baseball world. His miraculous productivity as a baseball coach, lecturer, radio and television sports commentator, and author have inspired helpless unfortunates the world over.

When the supreme baseball honor (election to the Hall of Fame) was bestowed upon Roy Campanella at the age of 47, it was recalled that he often said, "You have to be a man to be a big-leaguer, but you have to have a lot of little boy in you, too." He was unquestionably both.

Though he played in the big leagues for only ten years, super-catcher Roy Campanella will be remembered as long as baseball is played.

GORDON ["Mickey"] COCHRANE
He Always Came to Play

Mickey Cochrane had so many attributes that it is hard to sort them. In his 14 years in the major leagues, he established himself as the fastest, smartest, best-throwing, and most fiery backstop in the game. Branch Rickey, the baseball genius who saw them all perform for diamond glory, once publicly declared, in admiration of Mickey Cochrane: "I don't know of any catcher in history who could outrun him. There has been no catcher who could outthrow him, and for all-around efficiency and hitting power, plus baseball sense, he tops them all."

He was a superb take-charge baseball hero. He proved that with his dazzling performances with the Philadelphia Athletics (three consecutive pennants and two world championships), with his acumen as playing manager of the Detroit Tigers (two pennants in a row and a world championship), and with an overall .320 batting average in a 14-year major-league career. For eleven successive seasons he caught 100 or more games, and he also captured the coveted Most Valuable Player Award for his fame.

It took a bean ball to end Mickey Cochrane's fabulous career as a catcher. Its untimely end came in an early game during the 1937 season, when Mickey Cochrane was 34 years old. Pitcher

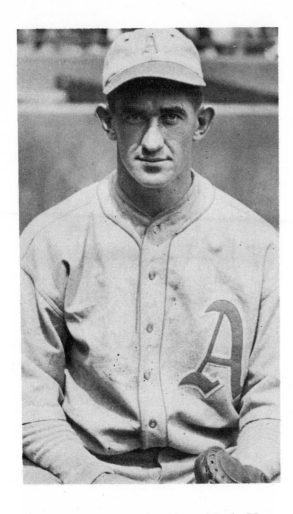

Bump Hadley of the New York Yankees beaned him with a fast pitch, and the Detroit Tigers' incomparable catcher was carried off the field with a fractured skull. Miraculously, his life was saved, but unfortunately, Mickey Cochrane never played again.

Born in Bridgewater, Massachusetts, Gordon Stanley Cochrane dreamed from boyhood on of becoming a big-league baseball player. His first taste of sports fame actually came as a star halfback for the Boston University football team. At that time he also played saxophone with a band to help him earn money to see him through college.

He was 20 when he heard that the Dover (Delaware) baseball club, which played in the Eastern Shore League and was a farm of the Philadelphia Athletics, needed a catcher. Until then, he had never tried catching. Nevertheless, Cochrane told a buddy: "If the Dover team needs a catcher, then I'm a catcher."

Cochrane did so well with the Dover team, showing such impressive finesse as a catcher, and hitting .332, that he was shipped to the Athletics' top farm club of the Pacific Coast League in Portland. There he upped his batting average to .333—credentials sufficient to bring him up to the major leagues, in 1925, when he was 22 years old.

In his first time at bat in the big leagues, as a pinch hitter, Mickey drove in two runs with a two-bagger, and also drove the regular catcher of the Philadelphia team to the bench.

For the next nine years, catcher Cochrane was the inspirational leader of the great Philadelphia Athletics teams, which won three pennants in a row (1930-'31-'32). The Philadelphia pitchers were superb in those years, but each one gave credit to Cochrane's heady work behind the plate, his smart signal-calling for the right pitches, his deadly efficiency in throwing out the best base-stealers in the league, and his catching of all kinds of foul pops. Mickey was on top of every play.

In 1934, during the country's Great Depression, when the Philadelphia Athletics fell into financial difficulty, fabulous catcher Mickey Cochrane was sold to the Detroit Tigers for more than $100,000, plus a couple of Tiger players. He became Detroit's playing manager. In his first two years there, Mickey's magnificent catching, powerful .300-plus hitting, and smart inspirational piloting led the Tigers to two pennants in a row—and a World Series championship, too.

Two seasons later came the tragic day when Mickey Cochrane was beaned and his brilliant catching career was suddenly ended. When he recovered, he came back to manage the Detroit Tigers for another season. It was only from the dugout.

Mickey Cochrane's record as one of the outstanding catchers of all time (1,482 games caught, 1,652 safe hits, 1,041 runs scored, and a lifetime batting average of .320) was enough to win for him top honors in baseball's Hall of Fame.

Upon his untimely death in 1962, at the age of 59, all his big-league contemporaries, and a legion of admirers who once had cheered for him, remembered him well—as the phenomenal catcher who always came to every game to play his best.

JOSH GIBSON

An Outcast From the Big Leagues

One of the saddest stories buried in baseball history is the tragedy of Josh Gibson, the folk hero who was robbed of his rightful glory as a superman of the diamond.

Though there is considerable evidence that he was perhaps the greatest catcher of all time, as well as the greatest slugger of baseballs who ever lived, he never played a single game in the big leagues—only because he was black.

It was not until a quarter of a century after his untimely death at 35 that Organized Baseball even acknowledged Josh Gibson's existence. He was ultimately elected to the Hall of Fame at Cooperstown—belated recognition by a game which had barred him from the major leagues all the days of his life.

Gibson was born at Buena Vista, Georgia, but spent his boyhood in the slums of Pittsburgh where he learned to play baseball so well that, at eighteen, he began playing pro ball in the Negro leagues of the time—the Twenties—first with the Homestead Grays, and later with the famed barnstorming Pittsburgh Crawfords. Though there were many fine players in the black leagues, Josh Gibson became the greatest of them all. He actually became a folk hero for his people. For that barrel-chested catcher became the biggest at-

traction of his race in baseball. His admirers and worshipers were legion.

There was no catcher on the baseball scene, even in the big leagues, who could backstop like Josh Gibson. He caught with such smooth and effortless ease that he could have sat in a rocking chair when toiling behind the plate. His throwing arm was like a rifle, and he often threw out base runners attempting to steal without even getting out of his crouch. He rarely made an error or a wrong judgment. His durability was astonishing. He played almost every day, summer and winter, barnstorming throughout the United States and Latin America. Often he played in as many as three baseball games a day.

He was a phenomenal catcher who could do everything possible behind

home plate. And when it came to hitting, the six-foot-four, 210-pound Josh generated unbelievable batting power. He hit a baseball for fantastic distances, even when he faced the best of the major-league pitchers in off-season exhibition games. One season he hit 69 home runs in Negro League competition, and another season he belted 72 homers. He never completed a single game in the seventeen years he starred as a professional baseball player without making at least a couple of safe hits.

But with all his fame, it was not enough for Josh Gibson to gain entrance to the big leagues, then a pure-white national pastime with figurative signs posted: "No Blacks Allowed."

Throughout his amazing pro baseball career, however, Josh Gibson still had only one dream: He hoped to be the first black ever to play in the major leagues. When that day came, in 1945, and it was the college-educated Jackie Robinson who was chosen for that singular honor, it all but broke Josh Gibson's spirit and heart. He had always expected to be tapped for that historic accomplishment.

Disappointed and sad, phenomenal catcher Gibson began to brood. He let himself go, began to drink heavily, and grew extremely fat.

Ironically, in 1947, only a short time after pioneering Jackie Robinson made his big-league debut, 35-year-old Josh Gibson departed from this world, the victim of a brain tumor.

For the following twenty-five years, Organized Baseball continued to ignore the prominence of baseball hero Josh Gibson. Finally, the wrong was righted. Though he had never played a single game in the big leagues, he was given his place in baseball's Hall of Fame, alongside all of the game's most distinguished players.

At long last, the outcast from the big leagues had for the ages a fitting last hurrah in tribute to his greatness.

FORREST ["Smoky"] BURGESS
The Pinchiest Hitter

It was the immortal manager, John J. McGraw, who introduced the pinch hitter to big-league baseball. In 1904, he astonished the major leagues by hiring Harry ("Moose") McCormick, a famous college baseball and football star of that time, for the sole purpose of pinch-hitting for the New York Giants.

Today, the use of pinch hitters in the major leagues runs to 4,000 or more a season. But the best pinch hitter that the big leagues ever produced was Forrest Harrill ("Smoky") Burgess.

Curiously, at the zenith of his fame, Smoky didn't even look like a ballplayer. He was a moon-faced little fat man who stood only sixty-eight inches tall. He weighed 200 pounds, much of it stacked around his waist. He was burdened with an ulcer, and hay fever. He always waddled up to bat on slow feet that constantly hurt. But he was the most gifted and deadliest clutch

hitter, and he collected more pinch-hits over a longer period of time than any other player who ever batted in the big leagues.

Born in Caroleen, North Carolina, Forrest Burgess was only seventeen years old when he became a professional baseball player. He had great expectations for fame as a catcher. However, until the age of twenty-two, he was lost in the minors before he finally made his appearance with the Chicago Cubs. But he did little backstopping for that team—he just wasn't good enough. Then, one afternoon in 1949, Smoky made his initial appearance in the majors as a pinch hitter. His first clutch hit was almost a home run.

The Cub manager soon recognized that his portly, broad-beamed little catcher, who was more of a butterball than a fireball as a backstop, possessed a talent not given to every ballplayer. Specifically, Smoky was an exceptionally gifted clutch hitter. He was the most confident batter who had ever stepped up to the plate to pinch-hit in an emergency. Thereafter, Smoky was rarely used as a catcher, but mostly as a pinch hitter.

As the baseball seasons passed, rotund and jolly Smoky drifted from the Cubs to the Philadelphia Phillies, then to the Cincinnati Reds, the Pittsburgh Pirates, and the Chicago White Sox. Wherever he went, he rarely worked as a catcher. But everywhere, he performed as a pinch hitter.

Often, he produced pinch-hits with stunning effectiveness. In 1956, when Smoky was with the Cincinnati Reds, that team came roaring into the final game of the pennant campaign with a chance to tie the all-time record of 221 home runs made by a major-league club in one season. On that final day, the Redlegs had 220 homers for their glory. But by the eighth inning, none of the regular Cincinnati sluggers had been able to produce the long homer that was needed to tie the all-time record. Finally, in exasperation, the impatient skipper of the Reds called on Burgess.

"Smoky, get up there and bat for McMillan," he snapped at the tubby clutch hitter. "But I want more than just another pinch-hit from you. I want a home run or nothing!"

"Yes, sir, homer or nothing!" said the unabashed Smoky by way of emphasis as he waddled out to the plate. The first pitch thrown to him was slammed over the outfield wall for a home run.

At times, he produced such spectacular last-ditch pinch-hit performances that his teammates would give him a standing ovation on his return to the dugout.

The most glorious day Smoky ever had was in July of the 1965 season. He was then with the Chicago White Sox, past thirty-eight, and there were sixteen big-league seasons already behind him. On that July 25, the White Sox were playing the Detroit Tigers. Late in the game, Ol' Smoky heard the call to come out of the dugout and pinch-hit. The bases were full, and a victory hung in the balance. On the very first pitch thrown to him, he lined a screaming double over third base, and he won another ball game for his team. It was the most memorable pinch-hit in major-league history, for he had broken a record that had stood unchallenged for three decades. It was number 108 for

Smoky, and with it he became baseball's all-time pinch-hitting champion.

Thereafter, every pinch-hit he made set a new all-time record.

When Smoky Burgess was past forty, he was still pinch-hitting and adding luster to his fame. At the end of the 1967 season he went out with a flourish as baseball's all-time clutch-swinger. He had knocked out 144 hits as a pinch-hitter—the most ever achieved by any major-league player.

HURLING WIZARDS

CY YOUNG

All He Did Was Win

Denton ("Cy") Young won more major-league games than any pitcher ever did, or ever will. Only he pitched for 22 consecutive years, winning an unbelievable total of 511 games.

Sixteen times he won 20 or more games a season, including 14 years in a row. Five times he topped 30 wins a season. He was the first big-league pitcher to hurl three no-hit no-run games, and only he ever hurled 23 consecutive hitless innings. While hanging up his many victories, he struck out 2,819 batters and pitched 77 shutouts.

The greatest of all big-league pitchers came right off the mowing machine on the farm where he was born at Gilmore, Ohio. He was 23 when he began pitching in professional baseball for $75 a month. At 24, he came to the big leagues to pitch for the Cleveland club, then in the National League. It was late in the 1890 season.

For Cy's debut the club provided the six-foot-two, 210-pound Cy Young with a uniform several sizes too small for him, and with patches in various places. He looked like the perfect hayseed. When "the big rube" walked out to the

mound, the fans, his teammates, the rival players, and even the umpires, laughed uproariously at the sight of him. But the laughter quickly died down when Cy Young started to pitch. He pitched a three-hit victory to begin his unprecedented career, and nobody ever laughed at him again.

Before his short rookie season came to an end, 24-year-old Cy Young had time to win only nine games. But the following season he had time to win 27 games, and the year after that he won 36 games. Then he continued to roll on as a winner beyond belief.

For eleven years he pitched for both Cleveland and St. Louis, then in the National League. And with the birth of the American League, he pitched for eleven more years for the Cleveland and Boston clubs. He became the first

to pitch a no-hitter in both major leagues. He was the first hurler in the 20th century to pitch a perfect no-hit no-run game. Cy Young was 37 years old when he accomplished that feat.

The ace right-hander had amazing durability as the winningest pitcher. He appeared in 906 games, made 818 starts, pitched 7,377 innings, and completed 751 games, to compile a fantastic all-time record of 511 victories against 313 losses. While doing all that, amazing Cy Young also made more hits than any other big-league pitcher in history—638—and scored 328 runs, also an all-time record for a big-league hurler.

Though Cy Young never was paid more than $5,000 a season, he was a baseball hero beyond reproach, and the soul of honesty. Gamblers once offered him $25,000 to let up a little on the mound for an important game. Angrily, he threw the men out of his hotel room, then went out and pitched one of his finest games for a victory.

He was 44 years old when, during the 1911 season, he decided to call it a career, even though his arm was as good as ever.

On a blistering hot afternoon, he lost a grueling 1-0 hurling duel to a sensational rookie who was half his age. Said old Cy Young after that defeat: "It's time to quit when the kids start beating you. Besides, the boys are taking unfair advantage of the old man. They know I've grown too fat to field bunts, so instead of swinging at my pitches, they are laying the ball down. When the third baseman has to start doing my work, it's time for me to quit."

Naturally, when the Baseball Hall of Fame came into existence, Cy Young was promptly honored with a place in this pantheon. He was 70 then.

But another significant honor was bestowed upon baseball's notable pitcher. In 1955, upon Cy Young's death at the age of 88, the "Cy Young Memorial Award" was established, to be given annually to the outstanding pitcher in each major league.

Thus he continues to be an inspiration to all hurlers. After all, a ghostly accolade from the "Old Master" is now the highest honor a major-league pitcher can win.

WALTER JOHNSON
"The Big Train"

One Sunday afternoon in the summer of 1907, a traveling salesman happened to stop off for a few minutes to watch a sandlot baseball game being played in Weiser, Idaho. He was so impressed by the hurling speed of one of the pitchers in that game that he lost no time alerting a friend who at the time was piloting the Washington Senators of the American League. Soon afterward the drummer's baseball discovery was hired by the Washington club, sight unseen, for the price of a railroad ticket from Idaho to the nation's capital, Washington, D.C. That was how 20-year-old Walter Perry Johnson, born on a farm in Humboldt, Kansas, to parents of German-Scotch ancestry, became a big-league pitcher.

The six-foot-one-inch, 200-pound farm boy was a hurler with only one

sweeping effortless delivery—a fast ball. He had a pendulum right arm which propelled a baseball toward home plate like a slingshot. In an era of trick pitching, rookie Johnson's hurling was an open book. Everybody in the ballpark knew what he would throw to a rival batter: It was either a fast ball or a faster ball. And all batters saw his pitches arrive at home plate in a blinding blur. He was the swiftest pitcher who ever delivered a ball.

His first incredible feat was accomplished in his rookie season when he hurled an entire three-game series within four days, allowing only nine hits, and winning all three games by shutouts. The farm kid was only getting a running start on the glory road. Whatever he accomplished as the game's most wondrous pitcher during his twenty-one years on the mound for the Washington club, he did alone, because the Senators were a chronic and mediocre losing team.

For twelve seasons he won 20 or more games, ten times in a row. Twice, he won more than 30 games a season (32 followed by 36). So overwhelming was his speedball pitching that he was dubbed "The Big Train."

The feats he performed for his immortality were beyond compare. In the 5,924 innings he hurled for an all-time league record, he struck out 3,508 batters. It's one baseball record that will never be equaled. He was the only pitcher ever to complete 531 major-league games, and the only pitcher to achieve 113 shutouts. Once, he hurled 56 consecutive scoreless innings, and it stood as an unmatched record for 55 years. One season, he ran up a winning streak of 16 games in a row, for an American League record that has never been topped.

Walter Johnson was the first big-league hurler to have a President of the United States come to watch him pitch an opening game of a new baseball season. It happened on April 15, 1910, when President William Howard Taft, in the nation's capital, performed the first ball-throwing ceremony. It marked the beginning of a tradition. Thereafter, it became the custom for United States Presidents to "throw out the first ball" on Opening Day. "The Big Train" was the baseball hero directly responsible for the start of this important and honored tradition.

Only Walter Johnson ever pitched the opening-day game of a new baseball season before four different Presidents of the United States, and he won an opener for each Chief Executive—Taft, Wilson, Harding, and Coolidge. The Presidents' favorite ballplayer was the only man ever to pitch as many as fourteen opening-day games, and only he ever won as many as nine, seven of them by shutouts.

The phenomenal right-hander became a baseball idol for an entire nation. His modesty, sportsmanship, and nobility of character were unique. He never feuded with players, argued with umpires, swore, smoked or drank. "Goodness, gracious, sakes alive!" was his most profane expression. Schoolboys as well as grownups worshiped him. In the nation's capital he became a living legend.

His loyalty to his team and legions of fans was unmatched. Once, on a day he had been billed to pitch, he came to the ballpark complaining of a sore arm. But because the ballpark was jammed to the rafters with thousands of fans who had come to see him perform his hurling magic, "The Big Train" decided to pitch for a few innings. Suffering pain, he not only hurled the full nine innings to win that game, but he pitched a no-hit no-run masterpiece.

He was 37 when the Washington Senators finally glorified his magnificent pitching by winning their first pennant. That was in 1924. When old Walter Johnson pitched and won the key seventh game, a 12-inning thriller, to make the Senators baseball champions of the world, so emotionally frenzied was the joy that grown men cried, and there

was dancing in the streets of the nation's capital. The following season, his superb pitching won a second pennant for the Washington Senators. At the age of 38, he won two games in that World Series.

He was 40 when a viciously batted ball struck him and severely injured his leg. It finally forced him to quit as a big-league pitcher. He left with an astounding total of 416 victories.

Naturally, he was enshrined in baseball's Hall of Fame as an immortal. And soon after, a high school in Bethesda, Maryland, a suburb of Washington, D.C., was named after him.

CHRISTY MATHEWSON

Baseball's First Gentleman

When Christy Mathewson was born on August 12, 1880, in the Pennsylvania farm town of Factoryville, his deeply religious parents hoped that he would grow up to become a minister. Instead, he became a famous baseball pitcher. He was the first college graduate to achieve stardom in the major leagues, the first authentic gentleman of the national pastime, the first professional baseball player to become a sports idol to all the young boys of America.

Christopher Mathewson was twenty when he came to the big leagues from Bucknell University. He was a curious

candidate for diamond immortality. At college he had been an honored scholar, the president of his class, and a member of literary societies and the glee club. A handsome, blond, open-faced, broad-shouldered six-footer with the appearance of an Apollo, he had also been a football and basketball star, and the best pitcher Bucknell ever had. His contract to play baseball cost the New York Giants only $1,500. He pitched for them for seventeen years.

He knew greatness right from the start. A self-taught pitcher, he nevertheless had everything a hurler ever needed —strength, intelligence, grace, stamina,

courage, confidence, and a fierce competitive will to win. "Matty the Great" became his big-league nickname.

Starting in 1901, over a period of thirteen years, he won twenty or more games each season, and did that twelve times in a row. Four times he won thirty or more games.

When right-hander Matty was on the mound, his control was almost unbelievable. In 1908, while winning thirty-seven games—the most ever won in a season by a National League hurler—in the 416 innings he pitched, he walked only forty-two batters. In 1913, he pitched 306 innings for twenty-five wins, yielding only twenty-one walks. In that season, he went sixty-eight successive innings without yielding a base on balls to a rival batsman. That impressive record for control pitching may never be matched.

When Matty the Great first joined the New York Giants, they were a last-place club. He pitched the Giants to five pennants. In 1905, when he appeared in his first World Series, he performed the greatest hurling feat in the history of this classic. Within five days, he not only pitched three complete games and won all three, but each was a shutout triumph.

During his glorious seventeen seasons in the majors, he hurled in 634 games, pitched two no-hitters, struck out 2,505 men, and won 373 games. No other pitcher in the National League ever won more.

However, Christy Mathewson's contribution to the national pastime was more than just imperishable pitching talent. He set a new pattern for the conduct of all baseball players.

When the scholarly, gentlemanly, courteous, soft-spoken Mathewson came to the big leagues, the game was in a rough-and-tumble era, consisting mostly of unschooled, foul-mouthed, hard-drinking, brawling rowdies. But he didn't descend to their level. Instead, by the force of his sterling character, he lifted players up to his. On and off the playing field, Matty the Great set the pace for refinement, dignity, courtesy, and sportsmanship of the highest degree. He didn't smoke, drink, swear, or brawl. As baseball's first perfect gentleman, he was the genuine aristocrat of the game. As a man of strong religious scruples, he never pitched on a Sunday. Clergymen and schoolmasters hailed him as a model for all to follow. Youngsters worshiped him for being the highest type of American athlete.

96

Christy Mathewson became not only the first authentic baseball hero for America, but also an ideal.

When the United States entered the First World War, although Matty the Great was then thirty-seven, he answered the call for military duty and served his country well. He returned home with his lungs weakened by poison gas, which made him an easy prey for tuberculosis. In early October, 1925, the once incomparable right-hander quietly left this world. An entire nation mourned him.

That Christy Mathewson will always be remembered as one of the very best pitchers who ever lived is certain. The inscription on his plaque in baseball's Hall of Fame reads: "Matty was the master of them all."

SANFORD ["Sandy"] KOUFAX
King of the Dodgers

Sandy Koufax was one of the strangest heroes in baseball. In the twelve years he pitched in the major leagues, his first six seasons marked him as a mediocre failure and a frustrated loser. But in his next six years, he blossomed out into a glorious winner and as sensational a pitcher as ever lived.

He was born in Brooklyn, New York, as Sanford Braun. When he was a child, his parents were divorced; and when he grew older, he adopted the name of his stepfather—Koufax.

Serious, well-mannered and shy, Sandy never wanted to be a baseball player. He loved basketball, and by the time he had graduated from high school, he was so outstanding a hoop star that he gained a basketball scholarship to the University of Cincinnati.

As a college freshman, he was persuaded to try out for the baseball team, only because his basketball coach also was the school's baseball coach. Although Sandy had played only a bit of sandlot baseball back home, and had been a poor fielding and weak-hitting first baseman, he nevertheless made the college team as a pitcher because he could throw a baseball with great speed. To his surprise, as a college pitcher Sandy attracted the attention and interest of a baseball scout and was offered a $20,000 bonus, plus a season's salary of $6,000, to pitch for the Brooklyn Dodgers of the National League. He was then only 19 years old.

When he came to the majors, rookie Koufax was a hopelessly wild thrower and ignorant of pitching techniques. In his first big-league season, he barely managed to win two games. The following season he was no better.

Embarrassed and discouraged, the serious and proud left-hander wanted to quit baseball. To encourage him to continue as a pitcher, the Dodgers raised his season's salary to $7,000. In

1958, when the Brooklyn Dodgers moved to Los Angeles, Sandy Koufax went along with the team.

In his first six years in the majors, Sandy won only 36 games, while losing 40. But with each victory and defeat, the solemn southpaw learned more..

On August 31, 1959, Sandy for the first time amazed the baseball world with an unforgettable feat. In a winning night game before 82,794 spectators, he struck out 18 batters in only nine innings.

On a sunny afternoon of the following season, Sandy again amazed the baseball world with an incredible strikeout feat. In a winning nine-inning game, he fanned 18 men and became the only pitcher in history to strike out 18 batters in a single game—twice, day and night.

In the 1961 season, the handsome southpaw won 18 games for the Dodgers, and it seemed that he was about to reach the plateau of greatness.

But early in the 1962 baseball season, after he had twirled his first no-hit no-run game in the majors and won 14 games, Sandy ran afoul of fortune. Because of a bruise on his left hand, his fingers turned numb and lost their sense of touch. Doctors gloomily told him that he had a rare circulatory ailment. After Sandy was cured, he was told he almost lost a finger on his pitching hand.

In 1963, Sandy astounded the baseball world by staging a remarkable comeback. He not only pitched his second no-hitter in the majors and fanned 306 batters to set a new all-time National League strikeout record, but he also won 25 games. His phenomenal hurling won the pennant for the Dodgers, and the World Series championship, too. In that post-season classic, Sandy set the all-time World Series strikeout record for a single game by whiffing 15 batters.

Sandy hurled his third no-hitter early in the 1964 season, but again he was unlucky. After he had won 19 games, he injured his left elbow while sliding into a base. It ended his pitching for the balance of that season. Then, to his horror, he discovered that he had traumatic arthritis in his left elbow.

With the start of the 1965 season, Sandy was resigned to live with his ailment, but remained hopeful of being a once-a-week pitcher for his team. Once again he amazed with wondrous pitching feats. Despite the handicap of an arthritic left arm that had to be packed in ice immediately after every game, he accomplished one of the most fantastic winning seasons ever achieved by a big-league pitcher.

He twirled a perfect no-hit no-run game to become the only pitcher with four no-hitters to his credit. He completed 27 games, and he won 26. In the 336 innings he hurled, he struck out 382 batters, setting an all-time major-league strikeout record for a single season. His incredible pitching not only sparked the Dodgers to another pennant, but in the World Series he hurled two vital shutouts to win the baseball championship for his team.

In all, his incomparable pitching sparked the Los Angeles Dodgers to four pennants. And to enrich his fame, he set a flock of astonishing World Series strikeout records.

In 1966, at the conclusion of his twelfth season in the major leagues, at the age of only 31, and though he was still then the highest-paid pitcher in history ($135,000 a season), Sandy Koufax turned his back on the game and retired. He didn't want to risk continuing to pitch while suffering the pain and torture of an arthritic elbow, perhaps resulting in a left arm unusable for the rest of his life.

He left the big leagues a legend in his own lifetime, based on an awesome hurling record. Of the 397 major-league games in which he appeared, he won 165, and only he ever pitched four no-hit no-run games. Only he ever struck out 18 batters in a nine-inning game— twice. Only he ever registered 10 or more strikeouts in a game—97 times. He was the only left-hander to hurl as many as 11 shutouts in a season. He pitched 2,325 innings and struck out 2,396 batters, becoming the only big-league pitcher to strike out at least one man in each inning he hurled.

No wonder Sandy Koufax, who had never wanted to be a baseball player, wound up in the Hall of Fame with the other immortals as a superman of the mound!

GROVER CLEVELAND ["Pete"] ALEXANDER

Alexander the Great

Even though Grover Cleveland didn't reach the big leagues until he was 24, he remained shining brightly for twenty seasons. When he finally bowed off the big-time baseball stage as a pitching wonder at the ripe old age of 44, he left behind him a list of astonishing accomplishments and records that still stand.

From the outset, he pitched like a veteran. In 1911, when the Philadelphia Phillies bought him from the minors for only $750, rookie Alexander was phenomenal. His debut as a big-league hurler was unique. The tall, freckle-faced, sandy-haired rookie won 28 games in his freshman year. No rookie pitcher has ever equaled that feat.

For the following six seasons, that rubber-armed right-hander who pitched with effortless grace, no frills, and little conversation, won 162 games for the Phillies. Three times he won more than 30 games a season, and once, almost single-handedly, he pitched a mediocre Philly team to a pennant. All of those feats earned him the sobriquet of "Alexander the Great."

Through the seasons he performed other wonders as a mound magician. Like hurling four consecutive shutouts and four one-hit games in a row in one season, for an all-time record; pitching and winning two complete games in a day, twice; and hurling 16 shutouts in a season, another all-time record.

Mighty Alexander, who performed his mound magic with a baffling side-arm curve, a blazing fast ball, and uncanny pinpoint control, got started as a pitcher on a farm in Elba, Nebraska, where he was born into a poor family

of 13 children, 12 of them boys. He pitched for town teams in total obscurity until he was 22, when he became a pro hurler for the Galesburg team in the Illinois-Missouri League. Though he won 15 games in his minor-league debut, his baseball career was almost ended before it started. Due to an accident on the field, he developed double vision. But the following season, when he went to Syracuse in the New York State League, his eye ailment miraculously cleared up, and Alexander won 29 games and pitched 13 shutouts. They were his credentials for moving up into the big leagues.

After his first seven years in the major leagues, Alex went off to fight for his country in World War I. He served in France, saw action in many bloody battles, and suffered from exposure to poison gas, which left him subject to epileptic seizures.

When he returned to baseball, Alexander the Great discovered that the Phillies had traded him to the Chicago Cubs, for they believed that his best days as a pitcher were behind him. No major-league club ever made a bigger mistake. "Old Pete," as they began calling him, celebrated his return by leading the National League with 27 victories, and in the following eight years with the Cubs he never had a losing season.

The Chicago Cubs gave up on "Old Pete" when he reached the age of 40, and it was a mistake for them as well. He drifted to the St. Louis Cardinals, where his effortless and matchless pitching helped them win two pennants and a World Series championship.

That was the unforgettable 1926

World Series from which Old Pete emerged a baseball hero. In that classic against the then-invincible New York Yankees for the world's baseball championship, the teams split the first six games. Two of the Cardinal victories were pitched and won by Alex, who supposedly was on his last legs. Then, in the seventh inning of the final game, with the Cardinals leading by a run, the mighty "Yankee Bombers" staged a rally, with two outs, and filled the bases. Up to bat came the dangerous slugger Tony Lazzeri.

Alexander, who had been peacefully dozing in the St. Louis dugout, resting from a wild celebration of the previous night, was awakened and summoned to the mound as a relief pitcher. Coolly and quickly, Old Pete struck out batter Tony Lazerri on four pitched balls, then silenced the Yankee bats for the rest of that game to give the St. Louis Cardinals their first World Series championship. The drama of Alexander's feat became a baseball epic to be reconstructed and retold through the ages.

Grover Cleveland Alexander was 44 when he pitched his last game in the major leagues. He had toiled in more games than any other pitcher in National League history—696—and won 373. No other National League hurler ever won more than Old Pete. His 90 shutouts is still an all-time league record. And he had registered 2,198 strikeouts. There were a slew of other records he left as a never-to-be-forgotten baseball hero. The Hall of Fame opened its doors to welcome him into enshrinement as a pitching immortal.

But, ironically, after his glorious career was over, life turned sour and mean for Old Pete, until his death at 63. He drifted aimlessly from place to place, unhappy, ill, penniless, friendless, and almost forgotten by a fickle baseball world that had once idolized and cheered him as Alexander the Great.

WARREN SPAHN
The Winningest Southpaw

Eagerly, he began playing competitive baseball when he was nine years old. Reluctantly, he quit playing big-league baseball when he was forty-five. By the end of his playing career, Warren Spahn of Buffalo, New York, was a baseball legend—the winningest southpaw pitcher in the history of the game.

Warren's long journey to immortality

actually began when his father, a wallpaper salesman, decided to train and develop him for the big leagues. Before little Warren had even learned the alphabet, his dedicated father, a semi-pro ballplayer, taught him how to throw and catch a baseball. By the age of nine, Warren was the star first baseman for the Lake City Athletic Club midget team. Before he was thirteen, he had been advanced to playing first base for the Lake City Athletic Club senior team, on which his father, Ed, played third base. The Spahn father-and-son infield combination was the talk of the Buffalo sandlots.

At South Park High School, young Warren switched to pitching and became so outstanding a left-handed hurler that he attracted the interest of a big-league scout. When he received an offer to play pro ball, he was ready and willing to become an instant school dropout. But, to his surprise, his father insisted that he at least complete his high school education before embarking on a baseball career.

Southpaw Warren Spahn listened to his father's advice. But upon graduation from high school, he decided to pass up college for pro baseball. He signed with the former Boston Braves farm club in the Pony League for a salary of $250 a month.

At the start of his pro career, he was plagued by misfortune. He tore tendons in his left shoulder, which sidelined him, and when he resumed pitching, a painful arm ailment forced him to quit again. No sooner had he returned, after a long absence, than he was greeted by a thrown baseball which broke his nose and disfigured him for life.

Spahn was 21 years old when he finally began to pitch for the Boston Braves, but before he could win even one game, he vanished from the baseball scene for almost four years. World War II was in progress and, together with many other young men, he was a soldier fighting for his country. Participating in the historic Battle of the Bulge, he was wounded.

In 1946, Sergeant Warren Spahn returned to the Boston Braves, decorated with a Bronze Star, a Purple Heart, a Presidential citation for bravery, plus a set of jittery nerves. It wasn't until he was 25 that he finally won his first game as a major-league pitcher. In that entire season he won only eight games.

The following season, however, the slender southpaw blossomed into a stylish pitching master of control, guile, and durability. He won 21 games, and he was on his way to greatness.

As the seasons passed, Warren Spahn, with his rubber pitching arm and workhorse stamina, accomplished the most amazing feats ever achieved by a left-handed major-league pitcher.

He won twenty or more games a season for a record thirteen times. No other southpaw hurler ever matched that feat. Eight times he led the National League in victories, and nine times in pitching the most complete games, setting an all-time record.

During his fabulous career, he started more major-league games than anyone in history—665. In all, he pitched a record 750 games. Sixty-three times he hurled a shutout victory, and he registered the most strikeouts ever achieved by a left-hander—2,583. In 1960, when he was 40, and the oldest pitcher in the National League, he hurled his first no-hit no-run game. The following season, he pitched his second no-hitter, while winning 23 games.

In 1965, when southpaw Spahn was 45, he finally came to the end of the line. By that time, not only had he earned more than a million dollars in baseball salaries, but he had carved his name and fame into history as the winningest left-handed pitcher of all time. The record of wins: 363 major-league games.

It was no surprise when hawk-nosed, southpaw pitching-wonder Warren Spahn was enshrined in baseball's Hall of Fame as an immortal of the game. He was the winningest lefty pitching hero of all time.

MORDECAI ["Three-Fingered"] BROWN

Three Fingers Were Enough

In big-league baseball, skill is always of paramount importance. Soundness of limb is an obvious requisite. Yet many physically handicapped people have played baseball well enough to make the major leagues. Of all those to make the grade, the most famous was Mordecai Peter Brown.

Brown was born on a farm in Nyesville, Indiana. While playing in the fields as a boy, he thrust his right hand into a corn-cutting machine an older brother was operating. The machine took away half of his index finger above the knuckle and left his little finger useless. Soon after that misfortune, he fell and broke the third and fourth fingers of the same hand. For the rest of his life he had to live with his crippled and gnarled hand.

Nevertheless, young Mordecai became a fair pitcher for a local amateur baseball team, and one day he made a startling discovery. His injured hand

enabled him to hurl peculiarly, because the stub of his index finger permitted him to put an unusual spin on a baseball. He practiced long and hard to develop the strange sharp hop that slipped off his fingers. When he was convinced that he was ready to pitch professionally, he went to the manager of the Terre Haute club in the old Central League, asked for a tryout, and was hired. He was then 26 years old.

Promptly nicknamed "Three-Fingered" Brown, he became so good a hurler that the following year, despite his handicap, he was in the big leagues, pitching for the St. Louis Cardinals.

After winning nine games as a rookie, Three-Fingered Brown was traded to the Chicago Cubs. He became the hero of a glorious time in baseball—the legendary era of Tinker-to-Evers-to-Chance. Whenever he pitched for the Cubs, the bewildered and bewitched opposition was everlastingly pounding the ball into the ground for baseball's greatest infield combination to scoop up for easy outs. Brown was a flawless fielder, himself.

In the nine seasons Three-Fingered Brown hurled for the Chicago club, he became not only one of the outstanding pitchers of his time, but also one of the wonders of baseball history. His pitching duels with the immortal Christy Mathewson, the winningest hurler in National League history, were legendary. Twenty-four times he faced "Matty the Great," and he conquered him thirteen times. Nine of these were consecutive triumphs. One of those victories was the never-to-be-forgotten playoff game that won the 1908 pennant. That season he became the first major-league pitcher to hurl four consecutive shutouts.

Six consecutive times he won twenty or more games in a season, and his highest mark was twenty-nine. He also acquired the reputation of being the Cubs' "Royal Rescuer," because of his willingness, courage, and ability as a relief pitcher. Standing 5 feet, 11 inches tall, and weighing 180 pounds, he always drew the toughest pitching assignments. Rival hurlers and hostile crowds never bothered him. Frequently, he would go to the mound without even a warm-up in the bullpen. He had a wide repertoire of pitches and amazing control. From his crippled but powerful right hand came the most baffling curves that ever hoodwinked batsmen.

In the nine years that he carried the bulk of the pitching burden for the Chicago club, the Cubs won four pennants and two world championships in five major-league campaigns.

Three-Fingered Brown pitched in the big leagues for four different clubs and for fourteen years in all. He hurled in 480 games, won 239, and lost only 130. The three gnarled fingers of his right hand were enough to make him one of the pitching wonders of baseball history. He was the first physically handicapped ballplayer to be enshrined in baseball's Hall of Fame.

CHARLES BENDER
The Indian Chief

Born in Brainerd, Minnesota, a full-blooded member of the proud Chippewa Indian tribe, Charles Albert Bender was the first Indian to gain imperishable fame as a baseball hero. No other American Indian ballplayer ever equaled his abilities.

A graduate from the once-legendary Carlisle Indian College, and for a time a student at Dickinson College, the well-educated Indian went directly from campus into the big leagues. He was only 19 when he made his debut as a pitcher for the old Philadelphia Athletics. From the outset, in his rookie season, 1903, he revealed his extraordinary talents. He pitched 29 complete games in 33 starts, winning 17. In time, he had winning streaks of 10 and 14 in a row, and he also hurled a no-hit no-run game for his fame.

In the fourteen years that he starred in both of the major leagues, Chief Bender, as he came to be known, was hailed as the best of the money pitchers. His magnificent clutch pitching for the Philadelphia Athletics, lasting twelve seasons, helped them win five pennants. In five World Series, he was the outstanding star in four of them.

In his time, the six-foot-two, 180-pound Indian was one of the best-informed men in the game. A born gentleman, he was also one of the nicest and kindest men to play in the major leagues. Whenever hostile fans heckled him by emitting falsetto war whoops, Chief Bender would walk close to the stands as he returned to the dugout, and good-naturedly retort, "Foreigners!"

Chief Bender terminated his brilliant 14-year pitching career in 1917. He left with a record of 208 victories, only 112 losses, and 1,600 strikeouts, acclaimed as one of the greatest pitchers of all.

There was no doubt about his prominence as an unforgettable baseball hero.

He became the first and only Indian to enter baseball's Hall of Fame.

BOB FELLER

The Fireballer Farm Boy

On April 16, 1940, 22-year-old right-hander Bob Feller reluctantly went to the mound to pitch the inaugural game of the season for the Cleveland Indians against the Chicago White Sox. It was a cold, gusty afternoon. The young man had complained of a stiff arm, and warned his manager that he expected to be knocked out of the box quickly. Nevertheless, he not only pitched the full nine innings, and won by a shutout, but he recorded a hurling feat never before nor since achieved by a major-league pitcher. On that memorable day, Bob Feller pitched the first and only no-hit no-run game to take place on Opening Day.

It all began for Robert William Andrew Feller when, as a high-school boy of 17, fresh off a farm in Van Meter, Iowa, he made his major-league debut as a "boy wonder"-pitcher for the Cleveland Indians. In his first start, he struck out 15 men. No other pitcher ever broke into the big time so auspiciously. Less than three weeks later, rookie pitcher Bob Feller struck out 17 batters in one game. And two seasons after his spectacular debut, he became the first modern big-league hurler to strike out 18 men in a nine-inning game.

As the seasons passed, strikeouts became the hallmark of his glory, and "Rapid Robert" became his nickname. It was reliably determined that he pitched a baseball at 100 miles an hour. Fifty times he fanned ten or more batters in a game to enrich his fame as the strikeout king of the majors. He became the first big-league pitcher to strike out as many as 348 men in a single season (1946). It's still an all-time record for a right-handed hurler.

Born the son of an Iowa farmer who once had harbored an ambition to become a professional baseball player, himself, but failed, Bobby Feller was only six years old when his father began teaching him how to pitch. The two of them held daily practice sessions in the cow pasture behind a barn, where Bobby learned to hurl a baseball with such speed that a fast pitch once broke three of his father's ribs. Before he was 14, Bobby was good enough to pitch for a local baseball team of grown men. At 17, he was pitching in the majors.

As a major-leaguer, he was truly magnificent. Six times he won more than 20 games a season—once, as many as 27. Three times, "Rapid Robert" pitched a no-hit no-run game for his fame; and 12 times he pitched one-hit games, for an all-time record.

A stickler for clean living and dedication, Bob Feller became not only the most fabulous and highest-paid pitcher of his time, but also a popular hero to inspire the youth of America. In 1941, when he was at the height of his fame as the majors' most phenomenal pitcher, he enlisted in the United States Navy to serve in World War II. Almost four years passed before he returned to pitch again. Upon his return to the Cleveland Indians, he was still the magnificent and mighty "Rapid Robert," strikeout king of the majors. In that 1946 season, he hurled 371 innings, won 26 games, and struck out a record 348 men.

Bob Feller was almost 39 years old when he quit pitching. Though he had lost 44 months of big-league baseball because of war service, he nevertheless wound up with 266 major-league victories, and 2,581 strikeouts, during the 18 glorious years he had hurled for the Cleveland Indians.

There was no surprise in the baseball world when Bob Feller's name was entered in the Hall of Fame to be remembered down through the ages.

GEORGE ["Rube"] WADDELL

The Irrepressible Clown

In a cemetery in San Antonio, Texas, a six-foot shaft of granite with a stone baseball on top can be seen. That unusual monument marks the grave of the strangest hero America's national pastime ever had. For, even though

he was one of the greatest pitchers in history, he also was the greatest "screwball." He was George Edward ("Rube") Waddell, whose like will never be seen again.

In 1897, he first came to the big time from Bradford, Pennsylvania—a tall, powerful, deep-chested, 21-year-old country boy. In the fourteen years he remained in the major leagues, he pitched for five different clubs, because managers wearied of his eccentricities and let him drift away for their own peace of mind. Only wise and patient Connie Mack could handle Rube with any degree of success. As a result, that ever-clowning, erratic left-hander pitched five and a half seasons for the

old Philadelphia Athletics; and despite his crazy capers, Rube Waddell averaged 22 victories a season, never with fewer than 200 strikeouts in any one of them. He won 131 games for Connie Mack.

Rube Waddell had awesome speed, bewildering curves, and amazing control whenever he wanted to pitch seriously. But pitching wasn't always his primary passion. Clowning, fishing, drinking, running to fires, and indulging in unconventional pranks were—and no pitching assignment was ever important enough to divert him from unpredictable impulses.

The Rube was wild about fire engines and fires. Often, during games, whenever he heard the sound of fire engines racing to some fire, he would disappear from the ballpark to run off and help fight the fire. Once, he carried six people out of a burning building.

He loved to march in parades and lead the band. Many times he vanished to do just that. On his way to the ballpark to pitch, he was likely to stop off somewhere for hours to shoot marbles with kids, or play sandlot baseball games with them. Once, when his pitching was needed most, he was finally found working in a sideshow, wrestling live alligators for two dollars a day.

It was not unusual for Rube Waddell to jump from a boat, fully clothed, just to win a dollar. To win a five-dollar bet, he once actually jumped from a three-story window. During a hot pennant race, he disappeared for all of ten days. He was fishing happily in a secluded place where nobody knew him as a big-league pitcher.

Training rules and curfew hours meant little to Rube Waddell, who spent most of his nights hunting for fun and laughs. He was the first major-league player to cause a manager to hire a private detective just to spy on him.

Even when he was on the mound pitching, he was an irrepressible buffoon. He would turn cartwheels going from the mound to the dugout. But whenever he wanted to pitch seriously, he was incomparable. Once, he pitched every game of a six-game series, and won five of them for his team. Another time, within a period of only fourteen days, he pitched eleven complete games. In the 1904 season, Rube became the first pitcher in the history of the American League to strike out 16 men in a nine-inning game. He also struck out a record 349 batters that year. The mark stood unmatched for 43 years. Despite all of his legendary antics on and off the field, Rube Waddell struck out 2,375 men, while winning 191 games during fourteen hilarious years.

In the spring of 1912, baseball's personified screwball showed himself to be a hero of a different sort. While Rube was visiting the town of Hickman, Kentucky, the Mississippi River overflowed, threatening to wash away the town. He stood in icy water up to his armpits for hours, helping the populace stack sandbags to stop the flood and save the town from destruction. As a result, he contracted a severe cold and a racking cough which developed into tuberculosis.

Only two years later, utterly wasted in body, he died—a victim of tuberculosis of the throat. He was only 37 when, on April 1, 1914, he passed from this world. Taking note of the date, some people considered it appropriate for baseball's most famous zany to bow out of life on the traditional April Fool's Day.

Rube Waddell had the last laugh on the baseball world. So impressive and memorable had been his pitching that he was enshrined in baseball's Hall of Fame as one of the immortals.

CARL MAYS

Branded a Murderer

Carl Mays was one of baseball's strangest and most controversial heroes. During his turbulent 15-year career in the major leagues as an outstanding pitcher, more words were written about him than any other player. But despite his fabulous achievements, he was denied a place of distinction and honor in baseball history because he once threw a pitch that became the only fatal pitch of record in the major leagues.

Born in Liberty, Kentucky, the son of a poor minister, Carl William Mays grew up on a farm in the Missouri Ozarks. He had a hard and unhappy boyhood. The death of his father forced him, at the age of 12, to do a man's work on farms to provide for his mother and her children. He had no time for school nor play. Though his early education was neglected, he studied by himself for many winters to become far above average, and somehow, he also learned to pitch a baseball. At 22, after three years of obscurity in the minors, he crashed the big leagues to hurl for the Boston Red Sox. He was unlike all the other pitchers in the majors, for he threw blazing and baffling speed balls—underhand.

In 1916, his second season in the majors, his 18 victories helped the Red Sox win a pennant. And two seasons later, as a 21-game winner, right-hander Carl Mays pitched the games that clinched the 1918 pennant and World Series championship for the Red Sox.

With his ever-growing fame as a major-league pitcher, however, Mays became a human storm center. Trouble followed him to tarnish his image. His departure from the Boston Red Sox in 1919 threatened to disrupt the entire American League. For when he asked to be traded, the owners refused. He gave them ten days to decide in his favor, and when they failed, the headstrong, outspoken Carl Mays disappeared.

Finally, he was swapped to the New York Yankees in the middle of that season, but he became the first pitcher in major-league history to perform under a restraining court order—in every city of the American League circuit.

Nevertheless, submarine pitcher Mays went on to win for the Yankees as many as 26 games in one season, and 27 games another season, and he pitched them to two consecutive pennants (1921-1922). He also set a World Series record of 31 consecutive innings without giving up a walk to a rival batter.

It was an irony of fate that Carl Mays' standing as a baseball hero should become marred by only one pitch. On the afternoon of August 16, 1920, Carl Mays went to the mound for the Yankees to pitch against the pennant-bound Cleveland Indians. In that game, the Indians' famous shortstop, Ray Chapman, came up to bat for his third time. He was the swiftest player in the league, and known as a tricky plate-crowder. Twice he had hit safely, each a two-bagger. This time, Carl Mays fired one of his blazing submarine balls, and somehow Ray Chapman stepped into it. The pitch struck him on the head and he fell to the ground with a crushed skull. Several hours later, he was dead—the first and only player to be killed by a pitched ball in a major-league game.

The horror of that accident shook the baseball world to its roots. Suddenly, Carl Mays became the most controversial and hated man in the major leagues. He was branded a murderer. Angry players and irate fans demanded that he be banished from baseball forever. The abuse and vituperation heaped upon him was almost beyond human endurance. But the saddened Carl Mays revealed a brand of courage rarely seen in competition. Stoic and silent in his own defense, virtually ignoring all of the cruel taunts from rival dugouts, he continued to pitch. He completed that unhappy season with 26 victories.

Though he had to bear the stigma of a killer from that tragic day on, Carl Mays continued to pitch for eight more seasons. In his final six years, he hurled in the National League for the Cincinnati Reds and the New York Giants. He completed his career with 208 victories and only 126 defeats. His winning percentage and earned-run average outshine the marks of a number of pitchers now enshrined in baseball's Hall of Fame.

For the rest of his life, Carl Mays had to live with the bitter memory of his tragic role in the Chapman incident. At the age of 79, before he died on April 4, 1971, he noted with painful sadness:

"Nobody, it seems, ever remembers anything about me except one thing— that a pitch I threw caused a man to die."

There never was a more unfortunate and tragic diamond hero than that great submarine pitcher, Carl Mays.

JOE McGINNITY
The Iron Man

Joseph Jerome McGinnity was the only baseball player who actually "schemed" his way into the big leagues and diamond immortality.

Born in Rock Island, Illinois, he became a minor-league pitcher at 22, but after a couple of obscure seasons as a futile loser, he quit as a failure.

He became a saloonkeeper in Springfield, Illinois, and for several years he pitched semi-pro ball on weekends to promote business for his tavern. While tending bar, ingenious McGinnity thought of a way to infiltrate big-league baseball. He had studied the ways of the successful pitchers and noted that all of them depended on blazing speed, so he concluded that what baseball needed was a tricky pitcher with a new delivery. Joe McGinnity practiced and developed a slow, baffling underhand pitch.

With that never-before-seen "submarine" delivery, McGinnity not only crashed the big leagues, at age 28, but remained there for eleven seasons, winding up in baseball's Hall of Fame as the immortal "Iron Man" Joe McGinnity.

In his first year in the majors, pitching for the legendary Baltimore Orioles,

baseball's first submarine hurler won twenty-eight games. The season after, he won twenty-seven games, and the season after that, Joe McGinnity won twenty-six.

However, during his third season, Joe McGinnity was suddenly kicked out of the big leagues because he had lost his temper. On that day in 1901, while pitching, he became enraged at the famous umpire, Tom Connolly. He stepped on his toes, spat in his face, and punched him. For that disgraceful exhibition, Joe McGinnity was expelled by the president of the league.

So many fans protested Joe McGinnity's exile from the big leagues, however, and so persistent was the pressure that he be given another chance, that eventually he was permitted to return, but only after he had paid a stiff fine and publicly apologized to the umpire he abused.

Having done so, Joe McGinnity, the first submarine pitcher in major-league history, came back to win thirty-one games in one season, thirty-five in another, and twenty-seven in still another pennant campaign. In his eleven years in the majors, he won a total of 247 games.

But the feat that stamped him as the most unforgettable and the greatest underhand pitcher of all time, as well as the "Iron Man" champion of the majors, was achieved during the 1903 season, when he was with the New York Giants.

On the afternoon of August 1, the Giants played a double-header. Joe McGinnity hurled not only the first game, but also the second game. Two complete games—and he won both games.

On August 8, the Giants again played a double-header. And once more "Iron Man" McGinnity pitched the first game, as well as the second. Again, he not only pitched two complete games, but he won both ends of that double-header.

On August 31, the Giants again played a double-header. Sure enough, "Iron Man" McGinnity pitched the first game, as well as the complete second game—and, amazingly enough, again he won that double-header. Thus, he became unique as a pitcher of the majors. To this day he is the only three-time pitcher of a double-header in major-league history; and even more unbelievably, he bunched his trio of double-headers not only in the same season, but in the same month! Joe McGinnity won all three double-headers he pitched.

"Iron Man" Joe McGinnity, baseball's first submarine pitcher, set an imperishable major-league record by pitching two games in one day, five times in all. He also set an all-time modern National League record for pitching the most innings in one season —434 in 1903.

Indeed, he was an incredible "Iron Man" pitcher. After his glorious eleven years in the majors were done, he continued to pitch in the minors for fifteen more years, until he was 54 years old.

CARL HUBBELL
The Meal Ticket

The most dramatic and unforgettable happening in the history of the annual All-Star Game between the foremost players of the two major leagues came in the 1934 classic.

Carl Owen Hubbell, the New York Giants' magnificent left-hander, struck out, in succession, Hall-of-Famers Babe Ruth, Lou Gehrig, Jimmy Foxx, Al Simmons and Joe Cronin. Those mighty hitters represented the cream of American League sluggers. That particular season they accounted for 140 home runs among them, and their lifetime major-league homer total amounted to 2,202.

Yet Hubbell, known as King Carl, or "The Meal Ticket," went through those fabulous five home-run sluggers like a hot knife through butter. Each of the mighty batters returned to the bench bewildered by Hubbell's pitching magic.

His performance was all the more incredible because the American League players, with their heavy hitters, were an overwhelming favorite to win. In the very first inning of that game, Hubbell entered the contest with two men on, nobody out, and the legendary Babe Ruth coming to bat.

Hubbell, whose masterful screwball

pitch was a thing of beauty, threw three straight to Ruth, and the immortal Babe took them all for called strikes. Gehrig swung at a third strike and missed. Then came Foxx, who did the same. On eleven pitches, King Carl struck out three of the most dangerous hitters ever known.

In the second inning of that historic

game, Hubbell continued to weave his pitching magic, striking out both Simmons and Cronin. For good measure, he also struck out the following batter, Hall-of-Famer Lefty Gomez. There was never a pitching feat like it before, and never one since, as the 48,363 spellbound fans at that All-Star classic were to attest the rest of their lives.

But as remarkable and memorable as that performance was, Hubbell had other superlative achievements to point to for his greatness as a major-league pitcher.

He set an all-time National League record by pitching 46 consecutive scoreless innings. Once, he pitched a no-hit no-run game, and another time, he hurled an 18-inning 1-0 shutout victory in which he gave up only six hits, struck out 12, and didn't walk a man. In the 1936 season, he won 16 games in a row before that season ran out on him. So, the following season, he extended his winning streak to 24 by winning his first eight games. It was, and still is, the longest winning streak ever achieved by a major-league pitcher.

Twice he was named the National League's Most Valuable Player, and three times his phenomenal pitching led the New York Giants to pennants. Whenever a particular game had to be won, Carl Hubbell was the pitcher to do it. That's why his nickname was "The Meal Ticket."

Born in Missouri, he grew up in an obscure town called Shawnee, in Oklahoma. He was a gaunt, hungry-looking cowboy when, at twenty, he began his professional baseball career in the minor leagues. For almost six years he drifted from team to team, pitching for seven different teams in all. Finally, in 1928, he arrived in the major leagues to pitch for the New York Giants. He quickly impressed the Giants' legendary manager, John McGraw, with his unique screwball-delivery, which mystified batters, and his amazing control. He hardly ever walked more than one man in a game. But he wasn't an outstanding winner in the beginning of his big-league career. Five years passed before he produced his first 20-game-win season. From then on, he won more than 20 games a season five consecutive times.

Sixteen years he starred for the Giants. He appeared in 535 major-league games, pitched 3,591 innings, and wound up with 253 victories. King Carl was forty when his royal reign as a pitching hero came to an end. Five years later, the baseball world enshrined him in its Hall of Fame as a never-to-be-forgotten pitching immortal.

RUBE MARQUARD

He Stopped at Nineteen

To the present baseball generation, the name "Marquard" may not signify anything of importance except a hazy reminder of an ancient pitcher from the long-forgotten past. But in the second decade of this century he set a pace for winning that hasn't yet been matched by any hurler in major-league history.

Born and reared in Cleveland, Ohio, the product of a prominent family, young Richard ("Rube") Marquard was in such a hurry to win fame as a baseball player that, before he was sixteen, he left home for a secret tryout with a bush-league club in Waterloo, Ohio. Since he had no money to finance that adventure and dared not ask his father for it, he bummed his way. For five days and five nights, he hitched rides and slept in open fields to reach his destination.

However, his trip was all in vain. He failed to land the pro pitching job he had expected, and he returned home disappointed and disillusioned. But his boyhood ambition to become a famous pitcher had not been dampened.

As soon as he was eighteen, he again left home to become a professional ballplayer, despite his father's strenuous ob-

jections. This time, he had his first contract in hand. It called for his left-handed pitching services in the minor leagues, hurling for the Indianapolis club of the American Association.

His father, who was the chief engineer of the city of Cleveland, was so angry with him for embarking on a pro baseball career that he told him:

"Son, you're disgracing my name. If you disobey me and go off to become a professional ballplayer, I don't ever want to see you again."

Sad, but stubborn and firm, young Marquard left home, saying in farewell, "Dad, I hope you'll forgive me, and, perhaps someday, I hope you will even be proud of me for what I've done."

He had a glorious beginning in the minor leagues as a southpaw wonder. In his first season with the Indianapolis club he pitched forty-seven complete games, winning twenty-eight of them. He also led the league in strikeouts. Although the slim, wrynecked left-hander was no country boy, they nick-named him "The Rube." Rube Marquard was so sensational a minor-league hurler that when he was only nineteen he was already in the big leagues. The New York Giants had purchased his contract for $11,000. It was a record expenditure, for that period, for a big-league rookie.

But in 1908, Rube Marquard had a horrendous beginning in the majors. In his debut, he beaned the first big-league batter to face him, the next two walked, and the fourth walloped a grand-slam home run. In his first three seasons in the majors, he won only nine games and lost twice as many. Because of it, he earned the odious sobriquet of "The $11,000 Lemon."

But cocky and confident Rube Marquard was a pitcher not to be denied his destined big-league glory. In 1911, he finally came into his own, and he made all the critics who had ridiculed him change their tune. He not only won twenty-four games, but his brilliant pitching helped the Giants win the pen-

nant. The following season, his twenty-six victories helped the Giants win another pennant, and his twenty-three triumphs the season after that helped his team win its third flag in a row.

As time went by, he performed other feats of glory. Once, he pitched a complete twenty-one inning victory, and another time, he hurled a no-hitter. But the feat he achieved in 1912 set him apart from all the other hurlers in modern baseball history. In that season, he set a pace for winning that none of the pitching immortals have matched to this day.

Southpaw Marquard pitched the opening-day game of the 1912 season, and won it by the lopsided score of 18-3. That opener victory started Rube Marquard on the all-time longest winning streak. Thereafter, whenever he pitched for the Giants, he won. He won five games in a row, went on to ten consecutive victories, then on to fifteen, sixteen, seventeen, and eighteen. Only after he had won his nineteenth game in a row was he finally stopped on his amazing march. It brought to an end the longest winning streak by one pitcher in one season in this century.

All in all, he pitched nineteen seasons in the major leagues, he won 201 games, and he helped his team win five pennants. And while tall, dark, and handsome Marquard was winning imperishable fame as a pitcher, he was setting the pace as the bon vivant of the majors. He became the most dashing and glamorous baseball hero of his time, and the best-dressed.

Before Rube Marquard was finished with major-league fame, the father who had disowned him for becoming a professional baseball player forgave him. He even grew so proud of him that he boasted about the feats of his famous son, the only big-league pitcher to win 19 consecutive games in one season.

Rube Marquard earned his niche in baseball's Hall of Fame as a pitching immortal of the game.

JAY ["Dizzy"] DEAN
"Dizzy Is as Dizzy Was"

The biggest, loudest, and most outrageous braggart to play in the major leagues was an incredible hillbilly from Lucas, Arkansas, who gained fame in the Thirties as Dizzy Dean. Combining rare pitching ability and the sheer force of his personality, he became the most conspicuous baseball hero of his time. He was also one of the most amusing and lovable screwballs around.

Born into poverty, Jay Hanna Dean in his early years had to toil as a cotton picker to survive, until he grew old enough to join the peacetime Army at sixteen. Somehow, he learned to pitch a baseball well enough to become a minor-league player at the age of nineteen. Before he was 20, the St. Louis Cardinals snared him to pitch in the big leagues.

He pitched—and won—one game for the Cardinals, but then the club decided to send Dean back to the minors

for another year of seasoning. He told the Cards' manager, "You're making a big mistake sending me away. This'll be the first time a big-league team lost 25 games in one day, 'cause that's how many games I'm going to win this season, wherever I go." He went to the Houston club and won 26 games for that minor-league team.

So, the St. Louis Cardinals brought pitcher Dean back to the majors, and he started off his first full season with 18 victories for a seventh-place ball club. He also led the National League in strikeouts. Then, in successive seasons, the amazing hick won 20, 30, 28, and 24 games, also winning the league strikeout crown in three of those years.

No wonder right-hander Dean, with matchless tongue that poured out a million words, began to discourse and brag about his hurling talents, and about his wondrous achievements, past, present and future. With brazen effrontery he billed himself as the world's greatest pitcher. It wasn't all just a boast. In his own zany way, he merely announced what he was going to do, then did it.

Before the 1934 season began, Dizzy Dean predicted that he and his younger brother Paul, who had become a rookie pitcher for the St. Louis Cardinals, would win 45 games for the team on the way to a pennant. The public was amused by his bragging. So, that season, "me an' Paul" won 49 games and the pennant for the Cardinals. Paul Dean, the rookie pitcher, won 19 games, and Dizzy Dean, the three-year major-league veteran, won 30 games while losing only 7.

Then, before the start of that 1934 World Series against the powerful Detroit Tigers, Dizzy blithely announced, "Me an' Paul will win all the games the team needs to cop the world championship." So, Dizzy Dean won two games, and his kid brother also won two games, to crown the Cardinals baseball champions of the world.

So fabulous a pitcher was Dizzy Dean at the height of his fame that, in his first five and a half seasons for the St. Louis Cardinals, he won 133 games and lost only 66, for a percentage of .667—a higher winning average than that of any modern-era pitchers now in the Hall of Fame at Cooperstown. In that brief period, he also struck out more than a thousand batters.

When colorful Dizzy pitched without clowning, he had the finesse of the best of them. His blazing speed balls were bewildering to the mightiest sluggers. Whenever he was in trouble, he just reared back and pumped the ball into the catcher's mitt for blinding strikes. He called it "foggin' it in."

Once, before a crucial game, he walked over to the rival dugout and informed the players that he would pitch nothing but fast balls all afternoon. They laughed at his rash promise. But he did what he said he would do, and won the game by a two-hit shutout.

Dizzy Dean never let anyone forget that he was the greatest pitcher in the game, not even his own manager. Once, before an important game, Hall-of-Famer second baseman Frankie Frisch (the playing manager of the St. Louis Cardinals) tried to tell Dizzy how to pitch to some of the hitters he was about to face. Dean stopped him short by saying, "Frankie, it don't look exactly right for an infielder to be telling the world's greatest pitcher how to win a game." Manager Frisch left the locker room in a huff while Dizzy roared with laughter. Dizzy won that game by a shutout, striking out 17 men.

Dizzy mixed his magnificent pitching with countless antics. His kooky capers on and off the field are legendary. At times, his dismayed club owner had to pay out good money for the trouble and damages Dizzy Dean's shenanigans caused in the pursuit of fun and laughs. All through his major-league career, Dizzy was a carefree hillbilly out for a joy ride on baseball's glory road.

He was an amazing workhorse-pitcher who would have hurled in the majors for many years—and perhaps won 300 or even 400 games—if he hadn't become a victim of ill fortune. While pitching in the annual All-Star Game of 1937, a vicious line drive struck him on his foot and broke his toe. Dizzy subsequently returned to the mound before his injured toe had fully healed. Favoring it, he pitched without taking his customary full stride, and thereby injured his right shoulder and powerful right arm. Bursitis developed, and Dizzy's pitching brilliance waned. He was only 26 when it all happened.

With his pitching magic almost all gone, Dizzy Dean was still a wanted property good enough to be traded to the Chicago Cubs for $185,000. He spent the remaining three seasons of his ten-year major-league career pitching for the Cubs, and he even helped them win a pennant.

The most boastful pitcher in major-league history left the big leagues when he was 30. He had pitched in only 317 games for a total of 1,962 innings, and he had won 150 games, spicing them with 1,155 strikeouts.

It was a record impressive enough to win for him the supreme honor for a baseball hero—enshrinement in Cooperstown's Hall of Fame.

As long as Dizzy Dean is remembered as the fantastic right-hander who once topped all modern pitchers in color and efficiency, he also will be remembered as the happy hillbilly who enriched the baseball world with countless laughs.

HOYT WILHELM

Savior of Pitchers

The pitcher who appeared in more games than any other in baseball history was the incredible relief hurler, Hoyt Wilhelm. In his nineteen years in the big leagues, he toiled for no less than ten teams, and it wasn't until he had celebrated his forty-ninth birthday that, reluctantly, he quit pitching. By that time, he had been in 1,045 games —the all-time record for a pitcher.

Curiously, Wilhelm didn't even enter the big leagues until he was 29 years old. In 1952, he came to the New York Giants, a hungry rookie in search of his first major-league job. He was a right-hander with a slender knobby look and a puzzling butterfly delivery which he called his knuckler. At his age, he had a sense of despair that he would ever make it big.

The fabled Leo Durocher, then manager of the Giants, proposed that rookie Wilhelm become a relief pitcher. Wilhelm had no objection, since he was grateful for any advice and ready for any chore that would help him stay in the big leagues. He had spent ten grueling years in the minors, waiting for a chance to enter the big time.

Rookie Wilhelm not only made the

Giants' team, but as a relief pitcher he became the sensation of the big leagues. In his freshman year he appeared on the mound in 71 games—an all-time record for a rookie reliever. He won 15 games, saved more than twice that many, and set a league-leading earned-run average of 2.45. It was only the beginning for Hoyt Wilhelm as a baseball hero.

Long before, it had all begun for him in his home town of Huntersville, North Carolina. A pitcher for his high school team, James Hoyt Wilhelm could throw a fast ball and a curve, but his prize pitch was a knuckleball learned from a baseball book he had bought from a mail-order firm. One day when teenager Wilhelm was barely past 17, he walked from his Huntersville home to Mooresville, which had a team in the North Carolina League, and got hired as a pitcher for eighty-five dollars a month. When the manager of that team, who was also its catcher, found it difficult to handle Wilhelm's baffling knuckleball, he forbade him to use it.

After winning ten games for Mooresville, young Wilhelm cut short his first season in the minors to join the United States Army and serve in World War II. For three years he saw combat and was wounded at the Battle of the Bulge. He returned home a decorated war hero and promptly resumed his career as a minor-league pitcher.

For seven more years he toiled in the minors, dreaming and hoping for a call that would beckon him to the big leagues. It finally came when he was 29, and Hoyt Wilhelm was on his way as the most indestructible and most durable relief pitcher of all baseball time.

In his first three big-league seasons, he rewarded the New York Giants well for their faith in him. He appeared on the mound in 196 games, saved more than half that number for the starting Giant pitchers, and set a remarkable earned-run average of 2.11. So valuable and matchless was his heroic relief pitching that he not only helped the Giants win the 1954 pennant, but also led them to a four-game sweep of the World Series championship. He saved and wrapped up two of those victories with scoreless relief pitching.

As time went by, however, the Giants permitted the aging Hoyt Wilhelm to drift away to the St. Louis Cardinals. Then Hoyt drifted to the Cleveland Indians, and from there moved to the Baltimore Orioles. The Orioles welcomed the wandering relief pitcher by making him a starting hurler. Amazing Wilhelm responded by winning 15 games and leading the American League with a 2.19 earned-run average —thus becoming the first pitcher to lead both major leagues in this vital category. As if all that wasn't enough, he also pitched a no-hit no-run game.

Four years later, the ageless relief pitcher left the Orioles for the Chicago White Sox. After a few seasons of saving ball games for them, Wilhelm went on to Kansas City for a spell, and that team in turn traded him to the California Angels, who later sold him to the Atlanta Braves. Before his time ran out, at age 49, he also toiled as a relief pitcher for the Chicago Cubs and the Los Angeles Dodgers. And wherever he pitched, he saved ball games for his team.

When he finally ended his career, right-hander Hoyt Wilhelm had acquired every important record in acknowledgment of his relief-pitching talent—most appearances on the mound, most innings pitched, most games finished, and most victories scored.

Most likely, never again will there be another pitcher to make 1,045 appearances on the mound in major-league games, nor a relief pitcher capable enough to win 135 games. Those will always be Hoyt Wilhelm's credentials for immortality.

ROBERT ["Lefty"] GROVE

Terrible-Tempered Ol' Mose

"Lefty" Grove was a superb left-handed fast-ball pitcher for 17 years in the major leagues. Yet he could have been up for 22 years and could have won a hundred more than his 300 victories if his minor-league owner had shown compassion.

Robert Moses Grove was born in Lonaconing, Maryland, and it was said that he was a direct descendant of Betsy Ross. Lefty quit school in the eighth grade and worked in the mines around home, in a silk mill, and in a glass-blowing plant, before he discovered that a man could get paid for playing baseball. At 17, he played with a town team in nearby Midland, and then with Martinsburg of the Blue Ridge League, until the Baltimore Orioles, then a minor-league club, bought his contract. He was just 20 and his fast ball jumped a foot.

But in those days a minor-league club owner could hold on to a player until a major-league team met his price, and the Orioles' owner set a high price on Grove. In five years with the Orioles, Lefty won 109 games, lost only 36, and led the league in strikeouts four times. Then the owner agreed to sell him to the Philadelphia Athletics for $100,-600, but Grove had lost five years as a big-league pitcher.

With the Athletics, as a 25-year-old rookie, Grove caught everybody's attention almost immediately. In his first year he led the league in strikeouts (and in bases on balls, too, for he was notoriously wild). By his third year he was recognized as a superstar pitcher. He won 20 games, a feat he was to accomplish for eight seasons. Nine times he led in earned-run averages, seven times in strikeouts. He led the A's to three pennants in 1929, 1930, and 1931, and he won four of his World Series starts.

The greatest season ever registered by a modern-day pitcher was Grove's in 1931. He won 31 and lost 4, had a 2.06 earned-run average, and led the league in strikeouts. But most amazing, the four games he lost that year were by scores of 2-1, 7-5, 1-0, and 4-3 (two of the defeats were in relief)—so he easily could have had a 35-0 won-and-lost record. He won his first 10 starts, lost 2-1, then rolled off 16 more in a row, tying the American League record. He was out to smash the record against the old St. Louis Browns.

The game was scoreless after six innings. In the seventh, with two out, the Browns got two cheap singles. The next batter lined to left field. But the regular left fielder, Hall of Famer Al Simmons, had been given the day off, and a rookie named Jim Moore was there. He misjudged the ball and the Browns got a run—the only one of the game—and Grove's streak was snapped.

Now, besides his blazing fast ball, Lefty was renowned for his temper. (Once he went up to the venerable manager Connie Mack and said, "Nuts to you, Mr. Mack." And the gentle-spoken Connie Mack snapped back, "And nuts to you, too, Robert.") On the occasion of Moore's misplay, Lefty tore down lockers in the clubhouse, ripped uniforms, and shouted words of abuse at Mr. Mack because he had given Simmons the day off. Later, Grove cooled down and made peace with his manager and teammates.

But after nine years as an outstanding pitching hero for the Philadelphia Athletics, owner and manager Connie Mack fell into serious financial trouble, and he began to trade away his greatest players. Lefty Grove wound up in Boston, hurling for the Red Sox, and he had eight more glorious seasons. But he still remained the pitcher with the hottest and fiercest temper in the major leagues. The Red Sox playing-manager, Hall-of-Famer Joe Cronin, drew quite a bit of Lefty Grove's tongue-fire because of fielding ineptness behind him whenever he pitched.

For most of the last half of the 1941 season, when "Ol' Mose," as his teammates called him, was 41 years of age, he had 299 victories. The big 300th triumph kept eluding him, but finally he made it, and it was his last major-league victory. He completed his 17-year career with 300 victories, flavored with 2,266 strikeouts.

When Lefty Grove reached baseball's Hall of Fame, at age 47, it became known that his won-lost percentage (.682 for 17 years—300 victories, 141 defeats) was the highest of any pitching immortal. Fiery temperament or no, he was quite a pitching hero for baseball history.

SATCHEL PAIGE

The Ageless Wonder

On a day in July, 1948, there came to the big leagues the strangest and most incredible rookie in history. He was a six-foot-three, skinny, languid, lazy-looking pitcher who walked like an amiable camel. He claimed to be 39 years old, but there was proof that he was at least 42, or perhaps even older. He had come to pitch for the Cleveland Indians, and it was a historic occasion—he was the first black pitcher in major-league history. He was the unbelievable Satchel Paige, already a legend in his lifetime.

Born in Mobile, Alabama, Leroy Robert Paige as a youngster carried baggage in the Mobile railroad station for a couple of dollars a day, and that was how he contracted the moniker "Satchel"—a nickname that would identify him for the rest of his life. He began playing professional baseball before he was 17, pitching for the Birmingham Giants. He hurled baseballs with blinding speed. Eventually, Satchel Paige became a gypsy pitcher, wandering all over the United States, Canada and South America for barnstorming black baseball teams. He also pitched for the big clubs of the National Negro Leagues—the Birmingham Barons, the Nashville Elite Giants, the Baltimore Black Sox, and the famed Pittsburgh Crawfords.

Year in and year out, summer and winter, the durable Satchel Paige pitched more than 150 games a year, averaging about 15 strikeouts a start, and winning about nine out of every ten games he pitched. At times he pitched as many as five games a week, and three games in one day. He pitched with no windup and no lost motion, from a standing position on the mound. He threw only two kinds of ball—hard and harder. Even when he faced famous big-league hitters in various exhibition games, they rarely saw his swift pitches when at bat, and hardly ever hit his smart and tricky deliveries with any kind of success.

Throughout a quarter of a century of professional pitching outside of organized baseball, the unbelievable Satchel Paige hurled about 3,000 games, won nearly all of them, threw about 300 shutouts, and some 55 no-hitters. He became the most famous black pitcher of all time. In his prime he earned about $75,000 a year as a barnstorming hurling-wonder.

But finally, the incredible Satchel Paige came to the big leagues for his last hurrah. He was the oldest rookie in major-league history. At the time, he may have been 39, as he claimed to be; or 42; or even older, for no one ever found out his real age. Regardless of his mysterious age, Satchel Paige, the first black pitcher in major-league history, was an instant sensation for the Cleveland Indians, then in pursuit of the 1948 American League pennant.

In his first three starts in the majors, a total of 201,829 frenzied baseball fans flocked to the ballpark to see the ancient Satchel perform his hurling magic. He won two of those starts by shutouts. He pitched and won six key games for the Indians, and saved a score of other games in relief to help them win the 1948 pennant. He wound up that season with the lowest earned-run average in the majors.

Old as Satchel Paige was when he finally broke into the big leagues, he remained in the majors for six years, appearing in 179 games for three different teams. Though he actually won only 46 games for his big-league fame, he saved as many games as a relief hurler.

When the big leagues were done with him, Satchel Paige returned to baseball-barnstorming, and by the time he finally quit pro hurling, he was at least sixty years old. It ended the most unbelievable durability and longevity saga ever recorded in baseball history.

Old Satch finally received his just reward for being the most remarkable pitcher who ever lived. He was enshrined in baseball's Hall of Fame as one of the true immortals of the game.

No baseball hero of his age, or any age, deserved that honor more, in testimony of his greatness.

DUGOUT GENERALS AND OTHER GREATS

ALEXANDER CARTWRIGHT
Father of Modern Baseball

Although the origin of baseball has been lost in a welter of claims and controversy, one fact is certain: The true "Father of Modern Baseball" was Alexander Joe Cartwright.

Born in New York City, he was in his youth an enthusiastic player of the then new-fangled disorganized game of baseball. He was a star pitcher. In 1845, when he was a bewhiskered 25-year-old engineer and surveyor, Alexander Cartwright organized the first baseball team in America—the Knickerbockers. His teammates were all white-collar fellow New Yorkers of high social standing. As their guiding spirit, Cartwright put the haphazardly played game on a solid footing as an American sport. It was he who drew up the first set of rules for baseball. It organized and established the game very much along the lines it is played today.

First, Cartwright revised and diagrammed the original playing field. He laid out the modern diamond, with the bases 90 feet apart. He ruled that a baseball team would consist of nine players to a side, no more and no less.

His rules also provided for three outs per side for each inning of play, and an unalterable batting order.

He eliminated the practice then in vogue of "plugging" or throwing a baseball at a runner to retire him. Also, he ruled that a pitched ball hit outside the range of first or third base was foul, and decreed that any batter missing a pitched ball three times was out.

His original and ingenious set of rules for the then-infant game of baseball were so sensible that most of them are still in force today.

The first competitive baseball game played in America under Cartwright's new rules took place at a summer resort in Hoboken, New Jersey, known as Elysian Fields, on June 19, 1846. The Knickerbockers played a team known as the New York Nine, composed of laborers and mechanics of in-ferior social standing. To make sure that all players engaged in that game followed his new rules, Cartwright umpired that game instead of playing in it. The Knickerbockers lost it by a score of 23 to 1.

Under Cartwright's rules, the game of baseball became organized, and it began to grow and blossom into a popular sport. In March of 1849, adventurous Alexander Cartwright, stirred by the California gold rush, set out on foot with a dozen friends on a 156-day trek to the California gold fields.

Along the way, wherever he went, he played and taught the game to mountain men and Indians, spreading the seeds of organized baseball across the length and breadth of America.

Shortly after he reached California, Cartwright lost interest in the lure of digging for gold. After playing a number of baseball games with prospectors and frontiersmen, he set sail for home on a vessel bound first for China. He fell ill on that sea journey, and was put ashore at Honolulu. While recovering from his illness, he found the Hawaiian way of life so attractive he decided to spend the rest of his days there. He became one of Honolulu's most respected citizens. Cartwright continued to spread the gospel and joys of competitive baseball until his death on July 12, 1892, at the age of 72.

Alexander Cartwright has remained one of the unforgettable men of baseball history, for he is in baseball's Hall of Fame at Cooperstown. Upon his bronze plaque is engraved the testimony of his imperishable fame. It reads:

Alexander Joe Cartwright—"Father of Modern Base Ball."

THE CINCINNATI RED STOCKINGS

The First Ten Pro Pioneers

The Cincinnati Red Stockings, baseball's first professional team, was so far ahead of its time—and so good—that it went through its first season undefeated in 65 games, and the following year extended that streak to a fantastic 91 consecutive victories.

The team came into being in 1869 when there was a national interest in the new-fangled game of baseball. But the teams of that time were composed of gentlemen "amateur" players of the upper class. There is no doubt, however, that most of these local clubs had been hiring certain players and pretending that they were being paid for positions in the business houses of the teams' various backers.

When a prominent lawyer in Cin-cinnati named Aaron Champion decided to organize a baseball team composed strictly of paid players, it was the first time a team had publicly admitted paying its men.

To organize his team, Aaron Champion hired Harry Wright, a London-born cricketer who had turned to baseball and was one of those getting paid for it. Wright, who was to become known as the Father of Professional Baseball, immediately began gathering pro players from the eastern seaboard, where the game had thrived for more than a decade.

He first signed his brother, George, as shortstop. George had been playing with a team in what is now the Bronx in New York City, and was a fine in-

fielder, well worth the $1,400 his brother gave him. Then Wright acquired Doug Allison, a catcher from Philadelphia; Asa Brainard, an excellent pitcher; and Fred Waterman, a third baseman from New York City.

Then came Andy Leonard, left fielder; Charlie Sweasy, second baseman, from Newark, New Jersey; Cal McVey, right fielder, from Indianapolis, Indiana; and Charlie Gould, first baseman, the only native Cincinnati player on the squad. Dick Hurley was a substitute. Most of them were signed at $800 to $1,000 for the season. Wright himself was paid $1,200.

Until this time, baseball teams had always worn the long trousers used by cricket players. But Harry Wright decided that knickerbockers would allow more freedom of action and dressed his players in short white flannel trousers and shirts. The uniforms were completed with red stockings, sewn by his wife, Mary.

Thus equipped, the game's first pro team took on all comers and began its remarkable streak. First, the Red Stockings mopped up seven local Cincinnati rivals, and then set off for the "established" East. En route to New York, they chalked up ten more victories.

Then they won their most impressive victory, a 4-2 triumph over the prestigious Brooklyn Mutuals, considered the outstanding team in the East.

Back in Cincinnati, a crowd of 2,000 people milled around in front of the old Gibson House awaiting the score as it was telegraphed by half-innings. When the victory became certain, the people set red flares and fired salutes. It was the high point of the season.

Then the Red Stockings visited Newark, Philadelphia, Baltimore, Wheeling, and Washington, D.C., winning everywhere. By this time, when they reached the United States capital, their fame was so widespread that the players were summoned to the White House to be received and honored by President Ulysses S. Grant. When the club returned to Cincinnati, there was a civic banquet in its honor, and the founder said, "I've been asked if I'd rather be President Grant or President Champion of the Cincinnati ball club—and I answered, 'I'd by far rather be the president of the ball club.' "

So the club rolled on. After its 65-0 record in 1869, it won 26 more straight victories at the start of the 1870 season. That made it 91 games without a defeat, and it appeared the Red Stockings were never going to lose.

But on June 14, 1870—one year to the day after their dramatic victory over the Brooklyn Mutuals—they faced another Brooklyn team, the Atlantics. Before an excited crowd of 20,000, enormous for the period, the Red Stockings and the Atlantics battled to a 5-5 tie after nine innings. Manager Wright would not settle for a tie and bade the game go on. The Cincinnati team did score two runs in the eleventh, but the Atlantics came back with three to end the incredible winning streak.

Subsequently, the team lost only one more game—in Chicago, late in the year—but even one defeat was enough to wipe out their magic. The team disbanded, and Harry Wright moved on to Boston, taking the Red Stockings name with him to use for the glory of another club.

The first super-team had been established, and professional baseball had been accepted, too. The feats of the Cincinnati Red Stockings never were matched—and undoubtedly never will be.

In the old clubhouse where the Red Stockings dressed, there was an old clock that ticked off the time. That clock is still in good working order and stands on the first floor of the National Baseball Hall of Fame at Cooperstown, New York, a gift from the family of Aaron Champion, who changed the face of baseball.

JOHN McGRAW

Little Napoleon of the Dugout

Born in Truxton, New York, the son of a poor Irish railroad worker, John McGraw had a most unhappy boyhood. He was only twelve when his mother and four of her children died of diphtheria. Grief turned his father into a cruel drunkard, who often beat him unmercifully. To escape from the miseries of his boyhood, unhappy Johnny played baseball. He would walk miles for a chance to participate in a baseball game.

He was barely sixteen when he began playing professional baseball. Before he was eighteen, he was starring for the most famous big-league team of his time, the legendary Baltimore Orioles. Only 67 inches tall, and hardly 150 pounds heavy, Johnny McGraw became famous as the best third baseman of his time. A quick-thinking, scrappy, and pugnacious spitfire at the hot corner of the infield, he was a speed demon on the base-paths, and a dangerous .300-plus hitter. In 1899, he compiled a .390 batting average which to this day is still the highest ever achieved by a big-league third-baseman for a single season. He wound up with a lifetime batting average of .334.

Almost from the start of his career, McGraw revealed a talent for leadership. Eventually, he became the player-manager of the Baltimore Orioles. But his incredible saga as baseball's greatest and most fabulous manager really began in the middle of the 1902 season, when he suddenly became the pilot of the lowly New York Giants, a chronic loser then wallowing in the National League cellar. He was then twenty-nine years old.

Manager McGraw quickly transformed the losing Giants team into a winner, however. In less than two seasons' time, he piloted the New York club to a pennant, winning two in a row. He remained the Giants' manager for a record thirty consecutive years.

Nicknamed "Little Napoleon of the Dugout," McGraw played the part to the hilt. He became a supreme baseball dictator, ruling his players with an iron hand. He did all the thinking for them. In the dugout he sat in a specially-built raised seat that looked like a throne. He glorified or discarded his players according to his whims. But he was an unexcelled developer of diamond talent. No manager ever sent more of his players to the Hall of Fame than tough John McGraw. At one time, almost every team in the two major leagues was managed by a one-time McGraw ballplayer.

During his fabulous thirty-year reign as the Giants' manager, John McGraw became the most colorful, the most dynamic, the most ingenious, as well as the most controversial, pilot big-league baseball ever had. As a pacemaker, manager McGraw had no equal. He enriched the game with many startling innovations. He was the first pilot in history to employ and use a pitcher strictly for relief hurling duty. Also, he was the first manager to use a pinch hitter in a major-league game. He was the first to give players a dignity in their trade, and he changed the face, manners and style of the game by elevating big-league baseball from a dingy boarding-house existence to the luxurious world of swank hotels for his players, and million-dollar baseball parks to play in.

He also became baseball's foremost good-will ambassador. Out of season, he toured with his team to foreign lands to acquaint their people with the glories of the game.

Tough John McGraw bullied, drove, and guided players to incomparable achievements. In 1916, he piloted the Giants to 17 consecutive victories, playing on the road. And before that season ended, he piloted his team to 26 victories in a row, playing at home. Both are still the all-time winning streaks for a major-league team and manager. He was the first manager in history to win four pennants in a row, and the first to win as many as ten pennants for his fame. No other manager ever won more.

On June 2, 1932, he suddenly resigned as manager of the New York Giants. His departure shocked the entire nation. Blaring headlines mourned the end of the fabulous John McGraw baseball era. Less than two years later, a worn, weary, and sick John McGraw was gone from this world—a legend to live forever.

Of all the baseball managers now enshrined in the Hall of Fame, John J. McGraw towers above all. Historians still speak his name with reverence.

CASEY STENGEL
The Left-Hander Who Went Right

Once upon a time there was a happy-go-lucky young man from Kansas City, Missouri, whose ambition was to become a dentist. At 21, he used his baseball skills to earn the money he needed to pay for his schooling as a dentist. He hooked up with a bush-league baseball club as an outfielder, and when he became convinced that there was only a dim future for a left-handed tooth-yanker, he switched his ambition to become a ballplayer.

Fortunately for him, after a couple of seasons playing in the lowest minor leagues, he was spotted by a big-league baseball scout who bought him as an outfielder for the old Brooklyn Dodgers of the National League for $500.

When 23-year-old Charles Dillon Stengel reported to his first big-league team, late in the 1912 season, he came into the clubhouse carrying all his worldly possessions in a paper bag, and

his entire fortune of $95 pinned to his underwear.

When he found his way into the locker room, a group of Dodger players were engaged in a dice game. Rookie Stengel was invited to enter the crap game, and when he did, he quickly lost his entire fortune. Before he could get over the shock of his first big-league misfortune, in walked the Brooklyn manager, saw him, and snapped at him: "Ain't you the rookie outfielder they bought? Find yourself a uniform—you're starting the game in center field this afternoon."

Garbed in an ill-fitting Dodger uniform, and without even a warm-up, Casey played his first major-league game. His debut was spectacular. He came to bat five times that afternoon, made four hits, walked once, stole two bases, and made several sensational catches in the outfield.

From an amazing beginning like that, it was no surprise that Casey Stengel quickly established himself as an outstanding outfielder. But he did much more for his fame. He became a celebrated buffoon and clown. His crazy capers on and off the field triggered countless laughs throughout the baseball world. Because of his hilarious antics, fun-loving Casey had to play for five different teams, during his 14 years as an outfielder.

But at times, amidst his constant clowning, he performed astonishing feats. With glove and bat, he not only helped the Brooklyn Dodgers win a pennant, but he also helped the New York Giants win two pennants. In the 1923 World Series, zany Casey personally accounted for two Giant victories with last-minute home runs—and once distinguished himself by running around the bases without a shoe.

He was 36 when his playing days ran out. He had played in 1,277 major-leagues games and collected 1,219 hits.

Casey Stengel vanished into the obscurity of the minor leagues, where he continued his career in pro ball as a player-manager. But at 43, Casey reappeared in the big leagues as a manager. He piloted two teams, but with each he was a failure. Each was a downtrodden team staffed with mediocre players. But Casey had his laughs, win or lose.

Tabbed as a managerial failure, Casey Stengel again vanished from the big leagues. But when he was 60 years old, he startled the baseball world by returning to the major leagues as the manager of the New York Yankees, famed as the greatest pennant-winning club in history. Clowning Casey at the helm of the proud and mighty Yankees was the biggest joke of that time.

But once Casey found himself managing a team staffed with outstanding players, he proved to the baseball world that he was a wizard. In the twelve years he remained the Yankees' manager, he not only became the first and only manager to pilot a major-league team to five pennants and five World Series championships in a row, but he also guided the New York Yankees to ten pennants and seven World Series championships. His winning feat ranks as the top managerial record of all time.

When mighty Casey had aged to 72, the New York Yankees set him adrift because of old age. But he didn't vanish from the big leagues. He switched to the National League and became manager of a newly organized team known as the New York Mets. He became the highest-paid pilot in major-league history, since by then, old, colorful and bizarre Casey Stengel was a baseball hero.

It was a memorable and hilarious time for him as manager of the New York Mets, for he found himself with a strange collection of misfit players—clowns, screwballs, and kooks.

His team became the losingest major-league team in history. In the four-and-a-half seasons he piloted the Mets, they lost almost 500 games. But manager Casey never lost his humor nor his gift for laughter. Colorful and lovable Casey made his chronic losing team the major-league team for the masses. More fans flocked to the ballparks to watch the Mets lose games in hilarious fashion than to see the foremost winning teams in both major leagues.

On the eve of his seventy-fifth birthday, manager Casey Stengel fell and broke his hip, which ended his managerial career. He went out of the game with 1,928 major-league victories and more than a million dollars.

When Casey Stengel was 76 years old, his incredible 54-year career in pro ball as a player, manager, clown and buffoon was properly and fully rewarded. He was enshrined in baseball's Hall of Fame with all the other never-to-be-forgotten immortals of the game.

CONNIE MACK
The Grand Old Man of Baseball

In baseball's Hall of Fame, Connie Mack is unique among all the major-league managers enshrined there. He established the all-time longevity record for big-league skippers: 53 years.

Born Cornelius Alexander McGillicuddy, in East Brookfield, Massachusetts, the son of a factory hand, he was a cobbler's assistant until he was 22, when he embarked on a professional baseball career as a catcher. So that his name would fit into a box score, he shortened it to Connie Mack. At 23, lanky, skinny, and tough as rawhide, Connie Mack reached the big time as a catcher for the Washington club. In all, he caught 664 games in the big leagues, and wound up as a playing manager for the Pittsburgh Pirates. A

broken leg ended his career as a major-league catcher, but it was the beginning of a most incredible managerial saga.

In 1901, Connie Mack became the manager of the Philadelphia Athletics in the newly organized American League. He remained their skipper for fifty consecutive years.

In all that time, he never wore a baseball uniform, but sat in the Athletics' dugout dressed in street clothes, a tall, gentle, soft-spoken tactician famed as a scorecard-waving bench pilot, manipulating his players on the field.

With skill, wisdom, understanding, patience, heart, and humor, Connie Mack developed some of the greatest teams known. He also developed some of the greatest players ever seen in the big leagues, since they share a place with him in the Hall of Fame.

Manager Connie Mack piloted his Philadelphia Athletics to nine American League pennants and five World Series championships.

Some of the teams were so mechanically perfect that victory became monotonous for the Philadelphia baseball fans, and Connie Mack had to break them up to start all over again. In all the years he managed the Athletics, he hardly ever spoke a harsh word to an erring player. "My goodness gracious!" was his strongest epithet when he was displeased. No manager became so nationally respected, admired and loved as tall, gentlemanly Connie Mack.

He stayed with his Philadelphia Athletics until 1950, when he was 88 years old. When he finally retired, he left with an incomparable managerial record. Only he in history had piloted a baseball team in 7,800 major-league games, and led them to as many as 3,776 victories.

Connie Mack died at 93, and an entire nation mourned him, from the President of the United States to the humblest citizen. He was, indeed, the "Grand Old Man of Baseball."

WILBERT ROBINSON
Jolly Uncle Wilbert

He wasn't the greatest or the smartest big-league manager in history, and the team he piloted didn't win many pennants. But Wilbert Robinson was unique, and there'll never be another one like him. In his own way, he belongs with baseball's super-heroes in Cooperstown's Hall of Fame.

Jolly, fat, and eccentric, he was a colorful earthy character with a friendly naturalness that endeared him to all his players and the baseball world. Unquestionably, he was the happiest major-league manager who ever lived, the only pilot who really "had a ball" doing it. Never worried, never troubled as a winner or loser, he piloted one team for eighteen hilarious years, not so much for glory, but strictly for laughs. Because he did, he enriched the game with a legend flavored with so much humor that the memory of him continues to glow with affection.

Born in Bolton, Massachusetts, the son of the village butcher, Wilbert Robinson worked at his father's trade in his early youth, but he also found time to play baseball. At 16, he was playing for a semi-pro team; at 19, he was starring in the minors as a catcher; and at 23, he was in the big leagues. A trim, skillful speedster, he became an outstanding catcher for the Baltimore

Orioles, and he remained in the big time as a star catcher for 19 seasons. Only he in big-league history ever achieved the batting feat of seven safe hits in seven times at bat during a nine-inning game. It happened on June 10, 1892. To this day, that feat hasn't been matched, and may never be.

After his playing days were over, curiously, the jovial, homespun, 40-year-old Wilbert Robinson returned to

new manager of the St. Louis Browns. He was their pilot for three winless seasons, before he switched over to the National League to manage the St. Louis Cardinals. For seven seasons, he remained their skipper with no great success.

In 1925, however, when Branch Rickey became a baseball executive and the business manager of the St. Louis Cardinals, he began to change the face of major-league baseball. He invented the "farm system" to enrich the Cardinals with a steady flow of experienced and finished young players from the minor leagues. And over the years, this "farm system," born of shrewd wisdom, intelligent planning, and a unique power to look into the future, produced for the St. Louis Cardinals so many outstanding players that they won nine pennants in less than twenty seasons.

In 1943, however, Branch Rickey left the Cardinals to lay the foundation for a new baseball dynasty. He became president and general-manager of the old Brooklyn Dodgers, now of Los Angeles. Again, he revolutionized major-league baseball with astonishing results.

In 1947, that visionary master builder defied the entire powerful Big League Baseball Establishment as no baseball man had ever dared do before. Against all opposition, advice, warnings, and fears, Branch Rickey tore down the racial barrier that had existed in major-league baseball since its beginning as an American sport. He brought to the big leagues the first black baseball player—a 28-year-old college-bred athlete named Jackie Robinson. Because Branch Rickey had the courage to make his unbelievable baseball dream a reality, the gates of big-league fame and fortune opened to all worthy baseball players, regardless of color, race, or religion. Because Branch Rickey had the wisdom and the foresight to look into the future for baseball's good, hundreds of black players have starred in the big leagues in the subsequent years, and a host of them became the greatest and highest-paid in the game.

With the first black players Branch Rickey hired to star for the Brooklyn Dodgers, he built such a powerful dynasty that the Dodgers won six pennants in only ten years.

But the "Great Mahatma," as he came to be known throughout the baseball world, had other revolutionary dreams for the game's welfare, growth and popularity. Years ago, he began to preach the need of spreading big-league baseball beyond the sixteen teams then composing the two major leagues. Many ridiculed his expansion plans to organize new teams. But again, Branch Rickey shook up the stuffy Baseball Establishment, and only because of him, there are now twenty-four teams playing throughout the United States and even in Canada.

When Branch Rickey departed from this world in 1965, at the age of 84, he had already become an awesome legend. He is now immortalized in baseball's Hall of Fame as one of the greatest of the game's heroes. As much as any man, and perhaps even more, Branch Rickey was responsible for all that major-league baseball is today.

BILL KLEM
The Old Arbitrator

The umpire in baseball is as old as the national pastime. The greatest and most famous of all was Bill Klem, who set the pace for all diamond arbitrators.

William Joseph Klem, born of German parents in Rochester, New York, on February 22, 1874, loved baseball as a youth. For a time he played professional ball, but when he hurt his arm, he turned to umpiring to stay in the game. His first job as an ump was in 1902, in the Connecticut League. Baseball umpiring was then a despised, miserable, dangerous, and ill-paid occupation.

Small of stature but big of heart and courage, Bill Klem was appointed a big-league umpire by the president of the National League after three seasons in the obscurity of the bush leagues. From the start he showed unusual pride and spunk.

In his first National League game, he rendered a close decision that displeased manager John J. McGraw, notorious as the most feared umpire-baiter around. To silence and discipline the "Little Napoleon" of baseball, umpire Klem ordered him out of the game.

The shocked manager raged at him: "You dumb squirt, I'll have your job for this!"

But the ump calmly replied: "Mr. McGraw, if it's possible for you to take my job, then I don't want it."

Bill Klem remained an umpire in the National League for the next thirty-

seven years, and he officiated in over 5,000 major-league games.

He started the practice of "getting on the ball" by crouching behind home plate to judge each pitch from right over the catcher's shoulder. He was the first umpire to "draw the line" in the dirt in dealing with argumentative and rampaging players. Any complaining player who ever dared cross umpire Klem's line in the dirt to argue a decision of his was promptly booted out of the game. He called himself "The Old Arbitrator," and his proudest boast was that he never called one wrong.

He became the most respected, the most famous, and the best-loved umpire in the history of the major leagues. He raised the standards for all umpires for better conditions, higher pay, more respect, and greater authority. To the baseball world he symbolized the game's honesty.

He was the only umpire to officiate in eighteen World Series—a record. He also became the first umpire to be honored by baseball fans with a special day, given only to the greatest and most popular stars in the game. On that memorable day, Bill Klem revealed that umpiring in the big leagues had been more than a job with him—it had also been a religion.

He died at the age of seventy-seven, leaving behind him numerous contributions to the profession of big-league umpiring.

The men in blue may still be the loneliest men in the baseball world, but they are no longer always unsung heroes of the game. Major-league umpires are now men of pride, dignity, standing, respect, and authority . . . all because Bill Klem put the job in proper focus.

CHRIS VON der AHE
"Hot Dog Chris"

Since big-league baseball began, the game has had numerous owners of the major-league teams. Some were so unusual and noteworthy that they are now in baseball's Hall of Fame. But one who never gained such glory was Chris Von der Ahe, the most bizarre, most colorful, and the screwiest major-league club owner in history. In his own fashion, however, he became a baseball notable never to be forgotten.

Chris Von der Ahe was a comical-looking, bulbous-nosed, prosperous German tavern keeper in St. Louis, Missouri, when late in the 19th century he suddenly and surprisingly and quite by accident became the owner of a bankrupt baseball club known as the St. Louis Browns. He knew nothing about baseball and had never even seen a big-league game played. But he lost no time in making his ball club the most colorful and talked-about team in baseball.

He turned his St. Louis ballpark into a weird playground. With baseball games he offered to the St. Louis fans such side attractions as glamorous girl trumpeters, brass bands, chute-the-chute boat slides from a high tower down to an artificial lake, a beer garden, and even a race track across the

street from the ballpark for horse racing before and after games.

His players traveled from their hotel to the ballpark in open carriages, drawn by beautiful white horses. He would lead his team onto the field in parade formation. Even depositing the box-office receipts became a special ceremony. After every game, club owner Chris Von der Ahe, protected by two armed guards, lugged the cash collected in a wheelbarrow to the bank.

He hired and fired managers at will. One season there were seven different managers to pilot his St. Louis Browns. In victory or defeat, club owner Chris Von der Ahe spent with a lavish hand. In 1888, when his team won the pennant, he spent $50,000 for a celebration party and bought a complete wardrobe for each of his players. He built an apartment for himself atop his ballpark to live in, and he had a life-sized statue of himself installed at the entrance to his ballpark. Buildings he owned were named for the stars of his team.

In 1893, club owner Chris Von der Ahe came up with an astonishing food novelty. He had a local baker devise a new type of white-flour roll with a juicy sausage inside. It was meant to be a tempting concoction of a quick meal to be sold at his ballgames for five cents. His novel invention of a frankfurter on roll caused a sensation in the St. Louis ballpark. Its popularity spread quickly to wherever big-league baseball was played. Eventually, the "hot dog" became somewhat of an institution of the national pastime. Today, its sale in ballparks and other sport arenas is big business, running into millions.

Club owner Chris Von der Ahe, who introduced the hot dog to baseball, had a sad end as a club owner. He lost his money, his ballpark burned down, he was swamped with lawsuits, he was deserted by his friends, and he was betrayed by other jealous major-league club owners of his time. He was forced to sell his St. Louis Browns for a pittance. He died in poverty, a broken-hearted man. His last wish was granted. The life-sized statue which he had proudly displayed in front of his ballpark was placed over his grave.

To this day, there hasn't been a more bizarre, more colorful, more ingenious club owner in big-league baseball than incredible Chris Von der Ahe. If nothing else is ever remembered of him, let it never be forgotten that he first brought to the game of baseball the hot dog!

SOME RECORDS OF THE GREATS WHO MADE THE MOST

GREATEST MAJOR-LEAGUE HOME RUN HITTERS
[Lifetime—500 or more]

Hank Aaron	720	Jimmy Foxx	534
Babe Ruth	714	Ted Williams	521
Willie Mays	660	Ernie Banks	512
Frank Robinson	552	Eddie Mathews	512
Harmon Killebrew	546	Mel Ott	511
Mickey Mantle	536		

GREATEST MAJOR-LEAGUE HITTERS
[Lifetime—3,000 or more hits]

Ty Cobb	4,191	Willie Mays	3,283
Stan Musial	3,630	Napolean Lajoie	3,251
Hank Aaron	3,520	Paul Waner	3,152
Tris Speaker	3,515	Cap Anson	3,081
Honus Wagner	3,430	Roberto Clemente	3,000
Eddie Collins	3,313		

ALL-TIME BIG-LEAGUE .400 HITTERS

Year	Player	Avg		Year	Player	Avg
1894	Edward Delahanty	.400		1920	George Sisler	.407
1895	Jesse Burkett	.423		1922	Ty Cobb	.401
1896	Jesse Burkett	.410		1922	George Sisler	.420
1897	Willie Keeler	.432		1922	Rogers Hornsby	.401
1899	Jesse Burkett	.402		1923	Harry Heilmann	.403
1901	Napoleon Lajoie	.422		1924	Rogers Hornsby	.424
1911	Ty Cobb	.420		1925	Rogers Hornsby	.403
1911	Joe Jackson	.408		1930	Bill Terry	.401
1912	Ty Cobb	.410		1941	Ted Williams	.406

ALL-TIME BIG-LEAGUE WINNING PITCHERS
[Lifetime—300 or more victories]

Pitcher	Wins		Pitcher	Wins
Cy Young	511		Tim Keefe	344
Walter Johnson	416		John Clarkson	327
Christy Mathewson	373		Eddie Plank	324
Grover Alexander	373		Mike Welch	316
Warren Spahn	363		Hoss Radbourne	310
Paul Gavin	361		Moses Grove	300
Kid Nichols	360		Early Wynn	300

146

IMMORTAL HEROES ENSHRINED IN THE NATIONAL BASEBALL HALL OF FAME AT COOPERSTOWN

GREATEST ALL-TIME BIG-LEAGUE PLAYERS

	GAMES PLAYED	HITS	BATTING AVERAGE
First Basemen			
Adrian Cap Anson	2,253	3,081	.339
Dan Brouthers	1,655	2,347	.348
Frank Chance	1,232	1,273	.297
Edward Delahanty	1,825	2,593	.346
Jimmy Foxx	2,317	2,646	.325
Lou Gehrig	2,164	2,721	.340
Hank Greenberg	1,894	1,628	.313
George Kelly	1,622	1,778	.297
George Sisler	2,055	2,812	.340
Bill Terry	1,721	2,193	.341
Second Basemen			
Eddie Collins	2,826	3,313	.333
Johnny Evers	1,776	1,569	.270
Frank Frisch	2,311	2,880	.316
Charles Gehringer	2,323	2,839	.321
Rogers Hornsby	2,259	2,930	.358
Napoleon Lajoie	2,475	3,251	.339
Jackie Robinson	1,382	1,518	.311
Third Basemen			
John Baker	1,575	1,838	.307
Jimmy Collins	1,718	1,999	.294
Harold Traynor	1,941	2,416	.320

	GAMES PLAYED	HITS	BATTING AVERAGE
Shortstops			
Luke Appling	2,422	2,749	.310
David Bancroft	1,913	2,004	.279
Joe Cronin	2,124	2,285	.302
Hugh Jennings	1,264	1,520	.314
Rabbit Maranville	2,670	2,605	.258
Joe Tinker	1,641	1,565	.264
Honus Wagner	2,785	3,430	.329
Bobby Wallace	2,369	2,308	.267
John Ward	1,810	2,151	.283
George Wright	315	364	.251
Left Fielders			
Jesse Burkett	2,063	2,872	.342
Fred Clarke	2,204	2,703	.315
Ed Delahanty	1,625	2,593	.346
Goose Goslin	2,287	2,735	.316
Chick Hafey	1,283	1,466	.317
Joe Kelley	1,827	2,244	.321
Joe Medwick	1,984	2,471	.324
Stan Musial	3,026	3,630	.331
Jim O'Rourke	1,750	2,314	.314
Al Simmons	2,215	2,927	.334
Zack Wheat	2,406	2,884	.317
Ted Williams	2,292	2,654	.344
Right Fielders			
Roberto Clemente	2,433	3,000	.317
Sam Crawford	2,505	2,964	.309
Elmer Flick	1,408	1,764	.315
Harry Heilmann	2,146	2,660	.342
Harry Hooper	2,308	2,466	.281
Willie Keeler	2,124	2,955	.345
Heinie Manush	2,009	2,524	.330
Tommy McCarthy	1,258	1,485	.294
Mel Ott	2,730	2,876	.304
Sam Rice	2,404	2,987	.322
Babe Ruth	2,503	2,873	.342
Paul Waner	2,549	3,152	.333
Ross Young	1,211	1,491	.322

	GAMES PLAYED	HITS	BATTING AVERAGE
Center Fielders			
Max Carey	2,469	2,665	.285
Ty Cobb	3,034	4,191	.367
Earle Combs	1,455	1,866	.325
Kiki Cuyler	1,879	2,299	.321
Joe DiMaggio	1,736	2,214	.325
Hugh Duffy	1,722	2,307	.330
Billy Hamilton	1,578	2,157	.344
Mickey Mantle	2,401	2,415	.298
Eddie Roush	1,748	2,158	.325
Tris Speaker	2,789	3,515	.344
Lloyd Waner	1,993	2,459	.316
Catchers			
Yogi Berra	2,120	2,150	.285
Roger Bresnahan	1,410	1,251	.279
Roy Campanella	1,215	1,161	.276
Mickey Cochrane	1,482	1,652	.320
Bill Dickey	1,789	1,969	.313
Buck Ewing	1,281	1,663	.311
Gabby Hartnett	1,990	1,912	.297
King Kelly	1,434	1,853	.313
Ray Schalk	1,760	1,345	.253

	GAMES WON	GAMES LOST
Pitchers		
Grover Alexander	373	208
Charles Bender	212	128
Mordecai Brown	239	130
Jack Chesbro	198	127
John Clarkson	327	176
Stan Coveleski	216	142
Dizzy Dean	150	83
Red Faber	254	212
Bob Feller	266	162
Edward Whitey Ford	236	106
Pud Galvin	361	309
Lefty Gomez	189	102
Burley Grimes	270	212
Lefty Grove	300	140

Pitchers	GAMES WON	GAMES LOST
Jess Haines	210	158
Waite Hoyt	237	182
Carl Hubbell	253	154
Walter Johnson	416	279
Tim Keefe	344	225
Sandy Koufax	165	87
Ted Lyons	260	230
Rube Marquard	201	177
Christy Mathewson	373	188
Joe McGinnity	247	145
Kid Nichols	360	202
Herb Pennock	240	162
Eddie Plank	326	192
Hoss Radbourne	308	191
Eppa Rixey	266	251
Red Ruffing	273	225
Warren Spahn	363	245
Dazzy Vance	197	140
Rube Waddell	191	142
Ed Walsh	195	126
Mickey Welch	308	209
Early Wynn	300	244
Cy Young	511	313

Managers	GAMES WON	GAMES LOST
Charley Comiskey	822	534
Clark Griffith	1,491	1,367
Miller Huggins	1,413	1,134
Connie Mack	3,776	4,024
Joe McCarthy	2,126	1,331
John J. McGraw	2,842	1,984
Bill McKechnie	1,895	1,723
Wilbert Robinson	1,391	1,395
Casey Stengel	1,928	1,767